Doing Business in Developing Countries

Doing Business in Developing Countries
Entry and Negotiation Strategies

S. Tamer Cavusgil
and
Pervez N. Ghauri

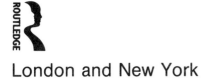

London and New York

658.049
C38d

First published 1990
by Routledge
11 New Fetter Lane, London EC4P 4EE

Simultaneously published in the USA and Canada
by Routledge
a division of Routledge, Chapman and Hall, Inc.
29 West 35th Street, New York, NY 10001

© 1990 S. T. Cavusgil and P. Ghauri

Typesetting by Witwell, Southport
Printed and bound in Great Britain by
Mackays of Chatham PLC, Chatham, Kent

British Library Cataloguing in Publication Data

Cavusgil, S. Tamer
    Doing Business in Developing Countries: negotiations and
    entry strategies.
    1. Developed countries. Foreign trade with developing
    countries   2. Developing countries. Foreign trade with
    developed countries
    I. Title   II. Ghauri, Pervez N.
    382.09172201724

    ISBN 0-415-04343-3

Library of Congress Cataloging in Publication Data

Cavusgil, S. Tamer.
    Doing Business in Developing Countries: negotiations and entry
    strategies/S. Tamer Cavusgil and Pervez N. Ghauri.
        p. cm.
    Includes bibliographical references.
    ISBN 0-415-04343-3
    1. Investments, Foreign–Developing countries. 2. Multinational
    business enterprises–Developing countries. 3. Foreign trade
    regulation–Developing countries. 4. Developing countries–
    Commercial policy. I. Ghauri, Pervez N., 1948–   .   II. Title.
    HG5993.C38 1990
    658'.049'091724–dc20   90–32348
                                                             CIP

To my parents, Niciye and Mehmet Cavusgil
To my parents, Iftikhar and Nasim Ghauri

Contents

Contents

Figures

Tables

Preface

*Doing Business in Developing Countries: Negotiations and Entry
Strategies* is aimed at Western business executives who are planning
to do business with Third World countries. Third World countries
represent increasingly important markets for Western businesses.
Yet they are not well understood in terms of their market potential,
business customs, political and social environments and negotiating
styles. Often we hear horror stories about unsuccessful encounters
between Western business executives and potential customers in the
Third World which are either private or government enterprises.
The market potential in these countries remains largely untapped.

This book fills an important gap in the business literature by
positioning itself as an authoritative and timely guide for business
executives, designed to equip them with the necessary knowledge
and skills required for successful international business ventures in
the Third World.

*Doing Business in Developing Countries: Negotiations and Entry
Strategies* will appeal to those business executives without sufficient
training in and knowledge about Third World markets. It aims to
provide the reader with a systematic approach to identifying,
negotiating and implementing successful business relationships
with customers from Third World markets. The orientation of the
book is toward carrying out effective and successful business
negotiations with counterparts from the Third World, and to design
effective entry strategies.

The book is illustrated with examples from actual cases dealing
with negotiations in areas such as the Middle East, South-East
Asia, China and Latin America. Business managers will find useful
information and advice in every chapter of the book.

It is hoped that the book will fulfill its promise of bridging the gap in providing an understanding of developing country market potentials, customers and environments. Equipped with such knowledge, the Western business person can develop appropriate strategies for negotiating and implementing profitable business transactions.

S. Tamer Cavusgil
Pervez N. Ghauri

Acknowledgement

Our thanks to Morten Bergquist for the cartoon artwork.

Chapter one

Introduction

Doing business with the Third World or developing countries requires a unique selling approach and thus is not an ordinary process. This is mainly due to the fact that Third World countries have different expectations from an international business deal. During an interview, Altaf Gauhar, Editor-in-Chief of the Third World-oriented *South* commented:

> We are interdependent – you need our raw materials and we need your manufactured goods and services in order to develop. But the costs of manufactured goods keep going up because of wage increases and inflation, while our prices keep falling because our economies are depressed. So we are being fleeced.

This remark reflects a major complaint of Third World countries. Gauhar pointed out the key global issues in the Third World's view as the following:

> The first issue is a negotiated arrangement that will reflect the needs of an interdependent world and give the producers of goods and commodities the feeling that the system is fair. Second, the reordering of priorities so that the social needs are the first consideration in allocating national and international resources. Third, the tremendous need for those who believe in democratic values to pursue them universally rather than pursue democracy only at home.
>
> (Moskin 1988:34–6)

The Third World concept

The World Bank has defined Third World countries as those with less than $7,300 annual GNP per capita. These include most of the countries of Asia (excluding Japan), Africa, the Middle East, the Caribbean, Central America and South America. These countries have been further divided into low-income economies with less than $400, lower-middle-income economies $400–1,700 and upper-middle-income economies $1,700–7,300 (annual GNP per capita). (See Figure 1.1.)

Industrialized countries including North America and Western Europe are often referred to as First World countries, while the Eastern bloc is referred to as the Second World. In this book the terms 'developing countries' and 'Third World' are used interchangeably.

Why consider the Third World for doing business?

More than 75 per cent of the world's population lives in the Third World. Also, Third World population growth rates are the highest of all nations (see Table 1.1). The population of the Third World in 1985 was 3.45 billion while that of the Western world was 737 million – and the population gap is widening. This is illustrated by Figure 1.2.

The Open Door policy of the Peoples' Republic of China (PRC) has enhanced the importance of these markets even more. One may imagine the effects of doing business in China, a market with 1 billion consumers, on firms like Coca Cola, Caterpillar, Electrolux and Ericsson, which have successfully established themselves in this market.

According to the *World Development Report* 1987, industrialized countries rely on expanding their markets in the Third World in order to increase their exports. The report estimates that imports from the Third World countries could reach $1.3 trillion by 1995. In most technology transfer projects, Western machinery and equipment are being bought by Third World countries. Moreover, while most of the production of manufactured goods still takes place in advanced industrialized countries, Third World countries, particularly the upper-middle-income economies, including NICs (newly industrialized countries), have become important customers for industrialized goods. Even the lower-middle-income countries are striving hard to build up their infrastructure and basic industries sector, for which they are importing Western technologies and components. In other words, while industrialized countries have

2

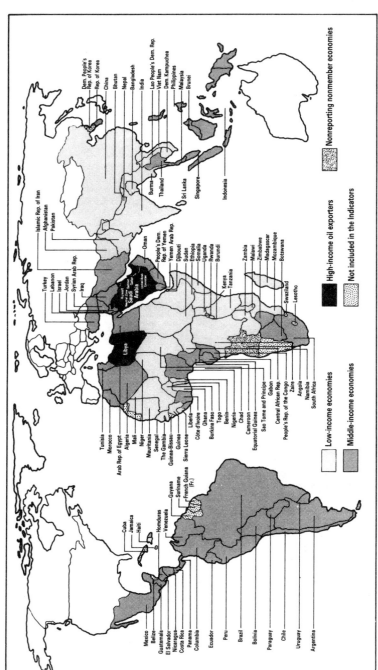

Figure 1.1 Map showing Third World countries

Dem. People's Rep. of Korea
Rep. of Korea
China
Bhutan
Nepal
Bangladesh
India
Lao People's Dem. Rep.
Viet Nam
Dem. Kampuchea
Philippines
Malaysia
Brunei

Burma
Thailand
Sri Lanka
Singapore
Indonesia

Islamic Rep. of Iran
Afghanistan
Pakistan

Oman
People's Dem. Rep. of Yemen
Yemen Arab Rep.
Djibouti
Sudan
Somalia
Ethiopia
Uganda
Rwanda
Burundi

Turkey
Lebanon
Israel
Jordan
Syrian Arab Rep.
Iraq
Kuwait
Bahrain
Qatar
United Arab Emirates
Saudi Arabia

Kenya
Tanzania
Zambia
Malawi
Zimbabwe
Madagascar
Mozambique
Botswana

Swaziland
Lesotho

Libya

Tunisia
Morocco
Arab Rep. of Egypt
Algeria
Mali
Niger
Mauritania
Senegal
The Gambia
Guinea-Bissau
Guinea
Sierra Leone
Liberia
Côte d'Ivoire
Ghana
Burkina Faso
Togo
Benin
Nigeria
Chad
Cameroon
Equatorial Guinea
Sao Tome and Principe
Gabon
Central African Rep.
People's Rep. of the Congo
Zaire
Angola
Namibia
South Africa

Cuba
Jamaica
Haiti

Honduras
Venezuela
Guyana
Suriname
French Guiana (Fr.)

Mexico
Belize
Guatemala
El Salvador
Nicaragua
Costa Rica
Panama
Columbia
Ecuador
Peru
Brazil
Bolivia
Paraguay
Chile
Uruguay
Argentina

Nonreporting nonmember economies

High-income oil exporters

Not included in the Indicators

Low-income economies

Middle-income economies

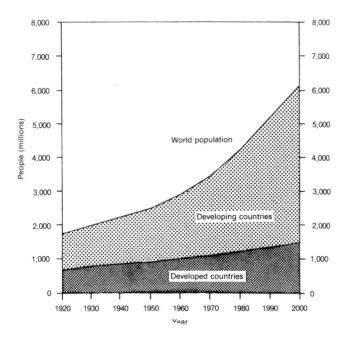

Figure 1.2 Population trends in developing and developed countries
Source: World Development Report 1987, IBRD/World Bank Statistics

most of the production of manufactured goods, Third World countries represent a substantial and growing market for capital goods and for industrial components.

Figure 1.3 shows the flow of foreign direct investment in developing countries and the countries which provide them. One can see that Western countries are the major source for inflow of direct investment. Exports from Third World countries declined from 31 per cent of total world trade in 1950 to 16.4 per cent in 1972.

Figure 1.4 illustrates the interdependence between countries of the First World and countries of the Third World.

The risk factor in the Third World

Until recently, First World firms have been hesitant to do business with the Third World, considering it to be too risky. International

Table 1.1 Population growth, 1965–85 and projected to year 2000

County group	1985 population (millions)	Average annual growth (per cent)				
		1965–73	1973–80	1980–5	1985–90	1900–200
Developing countries	3,451	2.5	2.1	2.0	2.0	1.8
Low-income countries	2,323	2.6	2.0	1.9	1.9	1.7
Middle-income countries	1,128	2.4	2.4	2.3	2.3	2.0
Oil exporters	461	2.5	2.6	2.6	2.7	2.8
Exporters of manufactures	2,048	2.5	1.9	1.7	1.6	1.4
Highly indebted countries	555	2.6	2.4	2.4	2.5	2.4
Sub-Saharan Africaª	385	2.7	2.8	3.1	3.1	2.9
High-income oil exporters	19	4.6	5.5	4.4	4.2	3.2
Industrial countries	737	1.0	0.7	0.6	0.5	0.4
Worldᵇ	4,207	2.2	1.9	1.8	1.8	1.6

Source: Wolrd Development Report 1987, Washington D.C.: IBRD/World Bank.

Note: a. Excludes South Africa.
     b. Excludes non-market industrial economies.

incidents such as the revolutions in Iran, Cuba and some Central American countries partially caused this cautiousness. However, considering the size of the market and the number of incidents, the political risk discussion is rather superficial.

In January 1988, *Svensk Export*, a reputable Swedish journal, ranked forty-six developing countries according to the risks involved in doing business with them. Economic and political factors were considered and a rank-order scale was used to include the degree of risk (see Table 1.2).

Under economic factors, indicators such as GNP, inflation, debts, export/import ratio, dependence on raw material exports, and urbanization are considered, with a maximum total of 49 points. Under political factors (maximum total of 51 points) indicators such as racial/ethnic conflicts, geographical situation (conflict areas), type of government (dictatorship/democracy), support to the government by the masses, and the risk of civil wars are taken into account. Countries receiving more than 60 points are considered high-risk countries, those with 50–59 points comprise countries with considerable risk, those with 40–49 points have some

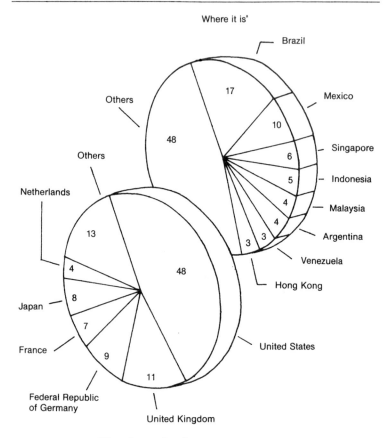

Where it is[a]

Brazil

Others

17

Mexico

Others

48

10

Singapore

Netherlands

6

Indonesia

13

5

Malaysia

4

4

Japan

4

Argentina

8

48

3

3

Venezuela

France

7

Hong Kong

9

Federal Republic
of Germany

11

United States

United Kingdom

Where it came from[b]

Figure 1.3 The stock of foreign direct investment in developing economies (per cent)

Source: World Development Report 1987, IBRD/World Bank Statistics

Note: Estimates have been rounded to the nearest percentage.
a. Based on IMF estimates for 1983.
b. Based on OECD estimates for 1982.

risk, those with 30–39 points represent very little risk, and countries scoring less than 30 points are no-risk countries. We will elaborate on international business prospects and problems related to the Third World in Chapter Three.

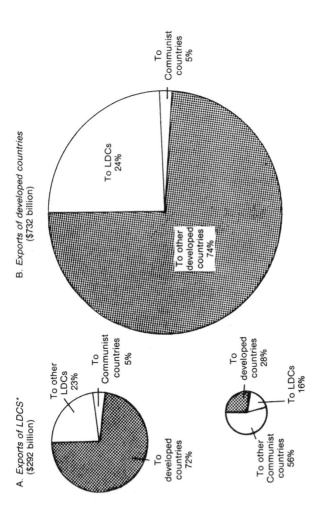

A. *Exports of LDCS**
($292 billion)

To other LDCs 23%

To Communist countries 5%

To developed countries 72%

B. *Exports of developed countries*
($732 billion)

To Communist countries 5%

To LDCs 24%

To other developed countries 74%

C. *Exports of communist countries* ($107 billion)

To developed countries 28%

To LDCs 16%

To other Communist countries 56%

Figure 1.4 Trade among the three worlds

Source: Yearbook for Trade Statistics, New York, United Nations, 1978. Cited in Kolde 1982:346
Note: *LDCs – Less Developed Countries.

Table 1.2 Classification of developing countries, illustrating economic and political risk

	GNP-progress	Inflation	Debts	Export/import ratio	Dependence on raw material	Urbanization	Ethnic conflicts	Geographical risk	Dictatorship/ democracy	Support of masses	War	Total
High risk												
Iraq	3	4	12	5	8	4	3	5	7	4	20	75
Angola	3	3	8	0	8	4	2	6	6	6	19	65
Sri Lanka	1	1	8	8	7	2	8	3	4	5	17	64
Ethiopia	2	1	7	8	8	1	5	3	7	5	14	61
Iran	0	2	2	3	8	4	2	6	8	5	20	60
Considerable risk												
Libya	8	3	7	0	8	4	1	4	8	5	10	58
Egypt	0	4	14	9	8	3	1	4	5	4	4	56
Nigeria	7	5	14	0	8	1	5	1	6	5	4	56
Panama	2	0	14	9	5	3	2	3	5	4	6	56
Cuba	2	3	14	9	5	4	1	3	6	4	4	55
Philippines	4	2	9	6	4	3	3	3	4	6	12	55
Chile	1	5	14	3	6	5	2	1	8	4	5	54
Morocco	2	2	10	9	6	3	2	3	5	6	8	54
Peru	2	5	14	2	6	3	2	1	4	5	8	52
Zimbabwe	3	2	8	4	6	2	4	4	5	5	9	52
Bolivia	4	5	10	5	8	3	2	1	3	4	5	50
Some risk												
Colombia	2	4	9	7	8	4	2	1	3	4	5	49
Yugoslavia	3	5	11	6	1	3	6	2	4	5	2	48
Tanzania	3	5	6	9	8	1	2	2	5	4	3	48

	Economic factors						Political factors					Total
Pakistan	0	1	7	9	3	2	3	4	5	5	8	47
Zaire	2	5	9	2	8	3	2	1	7	5	3	47
Argentina	3	5	14	0	8	5	1	1	2	3	3	45
Poland	1	3	14	4	2	4	1	1	6	7	2	45
Mexico	3	5	12	1	8	5	3	1	3	3	3	45
Turkey	1	4	7	7	3	3	2	3	5	4	5	45
Brazil	3	5	12	0	6	5	1	1	3	3	2	43
Hungary	0	1	14	5	5	4	1	2	5	4	0	43
Algeria	0	2	8	5	8	3	5	2	2	4	3	41
India	0	1	5	9	4	2	3	2	6	4	6	41
Kenya	2	2	7	7	4	1	1	3	2	5	3	41
Venezuela	4	2	14	0	8	5	3	1	5	3	1	41
Bangladesh	1	2	4	9	3	1	1	3	4	4	5	40
Ecuador	1	5	12	0	8	3	3	2	3	3	2	40
Nominal risk												
Indonesia	2	1	12	2	4	2	3	1	5	4	3	39
Kuwait	4	0	0	0	8	5	1	5	5	2	9	39
Tunisia	2	1	5	8	6	4	1	2	4	4	2	39
Camaroon	2	1	9	0	8	2	3	2	4	4	2	37
Saudi Arabia	5	0	0	3	8	5	1	3	6	2	4	37
Uruguay	2	5	7	0	5	5	1	1	4	4	2	36
Thailand	1	0	6	7	6	1	2	2	4	3	3	35
Malaysia	2	0	5	2	7	2	5	1	3	3	2	32
Rumania	0	1	7	1	4	3	2	1	6	6	1	32
No risk												
China	0	0	2	9	4	1	1	2	5	2	3	29
Hong Kong	1	5	0	5	1	1	1	2	1	1	1	19
Singapore	0	0	0	6	4	1	1	1	4	1	1	19
Taiwan	0	0	1	0	1	3	1	2	4	3	3	18

Source: *Svensk Export*, January 1988

Domestic versus international business

Domestic and international business involve similar types of activities, with the main difference being that in international business transactions take place in more than one country and market environment. The environment includes market structure, political and legal forces, economic forces, level of technology, structure of distribution channels, and cultural and social characteristics.

According to one author, marketing involves managing both controllable and uncontrollable elements as illustrated in Figure 1.5 (Cateora 1986:9). Uncontrollable elements are present both in domestic and international business. International business is more complicated, however, due to the level of these elements. Controllable elements are the internal decisions and marketing mix of the firm.

In Figure 1.5 the outer circles show uncontrollable elements of international markets, which can vary in different markets. Western businesses may find the uncontrollable elements of each foreign market complicated and compliance difficult. Moreover, these elements are very dynamic in nature, involving dramatic social, economic, political and cultural changes with increasing uncertainty.

This uncertainty can be reduced significantly, however, by studying carefully the operating environments of each country the firm is planning to enter. Some aspects of the international environment can be dealt with using basically identical marketing strategies, and experience in some regions can be helpful in addressing problems in another country.

Another dimension to be considered in international business is the political relationship between the domestic and foreign governments. The business executive going abroad must be aware of these relationships. In some countries of the Third World, for example previous British and French colonies, hostile feelings still exist, complicating the assessment of uncontrollable elements. Some countries arrange for special delegations to smooth the relationship at the government level in early stages of business relationships. The King and Queen of Sweden were among the first delegates for Swedish business firms when China opened its doors to Western firms and technologies. And in Brazil, when a large Swedish firm was competing for the contract to build an atomic reactor, negotiations were preceded by a visit from the King and Queen, reminding the Brazilian people that they were relatives (the Queen was born in Brazil).

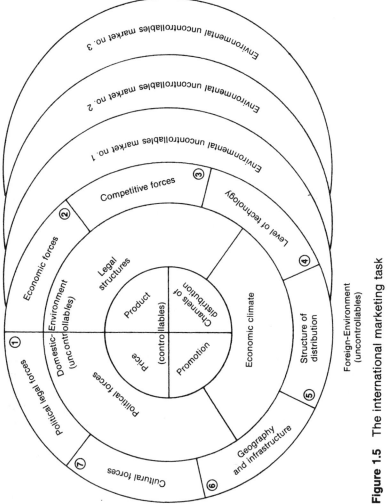

Figure 1.5 The international marketing task

Source: Cateora 1986:9

The diagram contains the following labels:

Environmental uncontrollables market no. 3
Environmental uncontrollables market no. 2
Environmental uncontrollables market no. 1

① Political legal forces
② Economic forces
Competitive forces ③
④ Level of technology
⑤ Structure of distribution
⑥ Geography and infrastructure
⑦ Cultural forces

Domestic-Environment (uncontrollables)
Foreign-Environment (uncontrollables)

Legal structures
Political forces
Economic climate

Product
Channels of distribution
Price
Promotion
(controllables)

The challenge of going international

One of the most significant trends of the past three decades has been the globalization of the marketplace. Previously isolated and protected markets such as China have been opening to competition from foreign firms. Thus, companies have begun to seek sales and profit opportunities in overseas markets with greater frequency, and the flow of products and resources across countries has expanded. This has had a marked impact on the lifestyles, incomes and values of customers, and on the structure and competitiveness of the marketplace in general.

The patterns of international markets are also changing. During the 1970s and 1980s, international trade has been moving more and more from raw material and agricultural products to manufactured goods and services. This is one of the reasons why industrialized Western countries' share of world trade has been increasing. These countries are the largest exporters, while Third World countries are the largest importers, of machinery and equipment as well as manufactured and semi-manufactured goods. Daniels and Radebaugh (1986) showed that developed countries increased their share of world exports from 45.9 per cent in 1948 to 64.6 per cent in 1972. However, after 1972 there was a discontinuity in this trend because of the oil crisis and higher earnings for oil-producing countries of the Third World, and the emergence of several newly industrialized countries (NICs) such as South Korea, Brazil and Singapore. NICs have taken over a considerable amount of trade from developed countries.

The following trends in the international environment are among the major forces behind the globalization of markets:

- Market environment – growth and wealth of nations have increased, due to successful industrialization efforts and the multiplied purchasing power of customers everywhere.
- Public policy environment – most countries have been systematically eliminating tariff and non-tariff barriers to trade since the Second World War. The General Agreement on Tariffs and Trade (GATT) and the establishment of the European Community have contributed to this trend.
- Resource environment – today it is much easier to conduct

overseas transactions since modern, sophisticated, convenient and economical forms of communication and transportation are available.

• Competitive environment – greater specialization among nations and firms has led to the development of many new products and services. A wide variety of consumer and industrial goods, services, knowledge and capital are demanded by overseas customers.

A number of historical, cultural and institutional factors have made Western (especially American) firms less 'export oriented' with respect to other industrialized nations such as Japan. Many managers do not consider exporting because they think it is too risky, complicated and not profitable. Others are simply indifferent to exporting and not willing to invest management time and money. Empirical evidence indicates that lack of information on foreign markets, buyers, marketing practices, competition, language, and unfamiliarity with the procedures of exporting hold firms back from exporting.

Developing markets abroad requires managerial and financial resource commitment. It is often necessary for firms to commit considerable management time, trained staff, and financial and other resources to develop practical marketing experience, distribution channels and a favourable image abroad before satisfactory benefits are realized.

Export assistance offered by Third World governments to encourage their own exports has adversely affected sales prospects of Western firms. In addition, tariffs, non-tariff trade barriers and other trade regulations imposed by these governments pose significant obstacles to these firms (Cavusgil 1983).

Firms often face difficulties in one or more of these historical, cultural and institutional dimensions. Table 1.3 identifies the stages of internationalization and primary impediments to exporting (Cavusgil 1985). Firms should overcome barriers at each stage before moving to the next stage in the export process. Research indicates that exporting needs vary according to the company's stage in the internationalization process. The firms at active or committed stages are more dependent on exports than the firms at non-exporting or reactive exporting stages. The exhibit also shows the kind of impediments in exporting faced by firms at different

Table 1.3 Illustration of company needs at various stages of export involvement

Stage in the export process	Profile of firms in this segment	Primary impediments in exporting
Non-exporter	Tend to be small, serving a limited domestic market. Not likely to possess any differential advantages such as a unique product or a patent. Not likely to be in a technology-intensive industry. Security oriented, risk averter management.	Not export capable or simply in-different to exporting
Indifferent/reactive exporter	Involved in exporting only to the extent of filling unsolicited orders. Suffer from uncertain/unfavorable expectations re the effects of exporting on company goals. No commitment to exporting in terms of systematic exploration, export policy or personnel.	Marketing management
Experimental exporter	Actively exploring export opportunities. Active in gathering export-related information from a variety of sources Favourable expectations re profitability of exporting. Management has high aspirations for growth.	Marketing research (informational)
Active exporter	Has greater stakes in exporting: export sales exceed 10 per cent of output. Usually experienced with respect to one or more export markets. Most likely to be in a technology-intensive industry possessing additional facilitating advantages.	Organizational goals and resources
Committed exporter	Foreign market opportunities receive equal attention and emphasis. Interested in entering additional foreign markets. Very favourable expectations of exporting and its effects on profits and growth. Regularly plans for export markets. Has a well-developed export structure.	Competitive and public policy

Source: Cavusgil in Murphy and Enis, Marketing, 1985:581

levels of export activity.

Doing business with the Third World brings with it several changes for the company. New tasks, unfamiliar environments and greater uncertainty all mean that the company needs to assume additional and greater risks. The job of international marketers is much more challenging than that of domestic marketers, not only because of the cultural disparities but also because of variance in the demand patterns, and the behaviour of firms and authorities in different markets.

Table 1.4 summarizes some of the challenges encountered by firms engaged in international marketing. First, there is geographic as well as psychic distance. The geographical distance makes physical distribution more difficult while psychic distance creates communication problems. Second, firms have to deal with multiple environments, such as public policy, traditions of trade, barriers to trade and competitive forces. Third, firms engaged in global marketing have to deal with multiple currencies and exchange rate variations; transactions in various currencies entail administrative costs and difficulties. Fourth, firms engaged in international marketing are often in conflict with their home governments as they take employment opportunities as well as other resources out of the country. These firms are also often in conflict with host governments with regard to remittance of their profits back to their home country or head office, ownership of local facilities and competition with local firms. Finally, cross-cultural interaction also creates challenges for international business persons. Differences in language, business customs and ethics, lifestyles and values, and other cultural dimensions often complicate business transactions.

Many authorities contend that Western business people are ill-prepared to conduct business in any culture other than their own. They are unfamiliar with the 'hidden dimensions' that frequently play a fundamental role in international business transactions. Different cultures require firms to adopt different behaviour patterns, since the strategies, structures and technologies appropriate in one cultural setting may fail in another. Therefore, one of the primary challenges of international business transactions is to operate effectively in a multicultural setting.

For example, in the Middle East a business person should have patience and an ability to haggle. Harding Carpets Ltd went to Saudi Arabia in the early 1970s to get a share of the wall-to-wall

Table 1.4 Challenges of global marketing

Distance

Separation of buyers and sellers by great geographic distance may create difficulties in communications and physical distribution. The exporter, for example, has to rely upon a larger number of intermediaries. These may include a domestic carrier, an international freight forwarder, a foreign distributor or agent, and local transportation companies. The delivery may take longer and the export transaction may be financed over a longer period.

Multiple environments

A company entering a foreign market is faced with a new set of public policy, competitive, resource and market environment constraints. Different political regions, barriers to trade, higher inflation rates, greater government involvement in economic affairs, limited availability of qualified distributors and advertising media, consumer illiteracy, and laws concerning termination of local distributors are just some of the environmental difficulties involved in conducting business with another country.

Multiple currencies

Apart from the administrative cost of handling transactions in various currencies, exchange rate fluctuations pose special difficulties. Exchange rates, the value of one currency expressed in terms of another, are subject to fluctuation as demand for various currencies changes. Therefore, quoting prices in the foreign currency or estimating profitability of an export transaction are difficult, especially for selling to countries that are experiencing high levels of inflation. Exchange rate risks are even more burdensome for MNCs that produce, sell, conduct R&D, and source factors of production in multiple countries.

Conflicts with home and host countries

On the one hand, home countries accuse their own multinationals of taking employment, R&D, and taxes out of the country. Some union officials have labeled the US MNC, for example, a 'runaway' corporation. On the other hand, the direct investment presence of a MNC in a host country makes it more vulnerable politically. Host countries may place restrictions on the operations of the MNC, such as limiting repatriation of profits. Or they may impose rules concerning use of local labour and materials, ownership of local facilities, or exporting of locally produced goods. Such restrictions are not limited to developing countries who desire to benefit from foreign investment. Recently, countries such as Canada, France, Japan, and Saudi Arabia have placed restrictions on the activities of foreign companies within their markets.

Social and corporate culture differences, business customs, and language

Stepping into a different social and cultural environment, the international marketer encounters one or more foreign languages, different values and beliefs, changing lifestyles and norms, varying aspirations, and motivations, and a new set of consumption, use, and shopping behaviors. These differences may have pervasive influences on all dimensions of international marketing including negotiations, product adaptation, design of promotional messages, and so on.

Source: Cavusgil in Murphy and Enis, *Marketing*, 1985:584

carpet market resulting from the high-rise building boom. Harding's policy had always been to offer the lowest price possible. However, no matter how fair the offer, the Saudis always asked for a rebate. Harding had to give a further rebate and ended up with a less attractive deal.

The extent to which a foreign firm will be affected by an indigenous culture depends on its level of involvement in the particular market. The greater the involvement, the greater the reliance on cultural growth and survival, and the greater the need for an understanding of the cultural environment.

The role of cultural variables in overseas business and guidelines for managers are discussed in detail in Chapter Seven.

The importance of negotiations

Previous studies conclude that Western firms are facing many difficulties in doing business with the Third World. Transnational firms, especially from Western countries, have difficulty understanding the needs, behaviour and evaluation criteria of Third World buyers. It is admitted that both parties have problems in negotiating projects and deals. Sound proposals which could have been beneficial to both parties have often been disrupted and dropped during negotiations (Ghauri 1983).

Ikle (1964:2) provided the basic characteristics of negotiations:

Two elements must normally be present for negotiations to take place; there must be both common interests and issues of conflict. Without common interests there is nothing to negotiate for, without conflicting issues nothing to negotiate about.

In other words, although there might be a number of conflicting issues, both parties would hope to achieve a common objective – i.e., both of them would want a transaction to take place. Therefore, negotiation is defined as an interaction process of resolving conflicts and reaching agreements to provide terms and conditions for the future behaviour of the parties involved (Ghauri 1983:16).

Little research has been carried out on international business negotiations despite the increasing importance of international business. In the past, the ability to negotiate was considered innate or instinctive, but recent studies have shown that negotiation as a technique can be learned.

More recently, as the result of studies conducted at the University of Uppsala, a network approach has been proposed. These studies claim that it is the social network which, in fact, influences the success or failure in international business (Johanson and Mattsson 1984). This approach suggests that firms should develop a network of relationships among suppliers, distributors, competitors and customers which serves as a barrier to newcomers or competitors positioned outside the network.

There are different kinds of networks. In social networks people from different firms and countries establish personal friendships which enhance the business relationship. A social network is most important in doing business with the Third World. Western firms should therefore try to establish a network of relationships in foreign markets. Another approach would be to locate existing networks, and by penetrating them handle some of the uncontrollables mentioned earlier. Many Swedish firms are very active in entering existing networks. Management looks for other Swedish firms working in the same market and asks them to introduce the firm to the existing networks of the new market. Firms not only obtain an introduction to the foreign market but also to the networks, thereby gaining access to influential people and related authorities in the particular market. This networking helps in negotiations and in the early stages of relationship development.

Organization of this book

The authors hope this chapter has convinced the Western business executive that developing country markets deserve special attention because of their potential and because of the unique aspects of doing business in such countries. The remaining chapters in the book build upon this foundation.

Chapter Two details alternative ways of tapping developing country market potentials. The business person needs to recognize that there are different options and trade-offs in becoming involved in overseas business.

Chapter Three reveals the 'promise' of developing country markets. The discussion documents the nature and characteristics of Third World customers and markets. A recommended approach to the marketing process is also offered.

Chapter Four provides an overall conceptual framework for

cross-cultural negotiations. This discussion elaborates on the key components to negotiations: background, atmosphere, process and outcome.

Building upon the conceptual framework presented in Chapter Four, Chapter Five focuses on the planning and management of the negotiation process. A strategic planning model identifies the stages of the process:

- The offer
- Informal meetings
- Strategy formulation
- Face-to-face negotiations
- Implementation

Helpful tips with respect to each stage of the negotiation process are also offered. Finally, Chapter Five addresses four key questions which concern firms getting ready for international business negotiations:

- How should management prepare for negotiations?
- Who within the firm should negotiate?
- What makes a good negotiator?
- What is a good outcome?

Chapter Six turns to the eventual outcome of international business negotiations: agreement. Distinctions are made between four principal types of agreements: sales/purchase, agent/distributor, licensing and joint ventures. Insights are provided as to how such agreements can be drafted and executed with developing country customers.

Chapter Seven offers guidelines for the firm doing business in developing countries not covered elsewhere in the book. These relate to the 'letter of intent', the role of government and local regulations, and the role of local intermediaries. Finally, this chapter introduces the concept of 'non-verbal communications' in international business and provides guidelines for managing effectively cross-cultural human interaction.

Finally, Chapter Eight offers some closing thoughts and recommendations.

Chapter two

Forms of participation in international business

Third World customers are very concerned about technology they import. They have preferences for 'appropriate' technology – the technology which is appropriate for a particular country in regards to its level of industrialization and availability of resources such as production factors. Countries attempting to reduce their unemployment rate prefer implementing labor intensive technologies. The investing country must be cautious in evaluating the pros and cons of its possible investment. Once a technological transfer is completed, the host country may not need the investor any more. Third World customers are anxious to modernize their economies through attracting technology-oriented foreign investment. India, for example, is trying to improve its ties with the U.S. for this purpose. Precautions must be taken against possible technology leakage to politically unfriendly countries. In India safeguards against leakage of technology to the Soviet Union must still be carefully enforced. In addition, India must guarantee that it will not use imported technology to build nuclear weapons or re-export to the Soviet Union. Still, U.S. companies are expanding their activities in India through many joint ventures. One of them is a $500 million project by Control Data to make mainframe computers

(Tefft, Javetski and Pitzer 1987:61)

Participation in international business requires comprehensive planning. Studies show that the entry strategy time span for most companies is from three to five years. This is due to the time required for managers to raise and answer questions regarding the direction and scope of their company's international business, and to achieve sufficient market performance. Finally, the company needs to make necessary arrangements to enter its products, technology, resources and management into a foreign country.

Several, often conflicting, forces determine a company's most effective form of participation in a foreign market, and both external and internal factors influencing this choice must be examined.

Factors influencing modes of participation

External factors

Market, production and environmental factors are some of the uncontrollables noted in Chapter One. These factors cannot be influenced by management decisions but they affect the selection of a particular entry mode.

1 Target market factors The present and projected size of target markets is a primary determinant for the type of entry. Small markets favour entry modes with a low break-even sales volume, such as indirect exporting, licensing or contractual arrangements. Large markets with high sales potential justify entry modes with a high break-even sales volume, such as subsidiary operations or joint ventures. Another dimension to be considered is the availability of suitable agents or distributors. If there is inadequate and/or inefficient marketing infrastructure the market may be reached only through a branch/subsidiary entry mode.

2 Production factors in the target market If production costs, such as raw material, labour, energy, etc., and the economic infra-structure (transportation, ports and communications) are favour-able, local production can be beneficial. Local manufacturing is not appropriate with high cost and poor infrastructure.

3 Environmental factors The economic, political and socio-cultural character of the target market can affect the choice of entry mode. Many products are luxurious in a market with a low level of economic activity or skewed economic activity, where most people live modestly or on a survival level. External economic relations exert influence on the choice of entry mode.

21

A persistent weakening of a country's balance of payments leads to import restrictions and/or devaluation of the exchange rate. In the last years of President Marcos, when the Philippines was facing a balance of payments crisis, the government restricted all imports. Even foreign manufacturing subsidiaries could not get foreign exchange to import their components. Finally, the government agreed that foreign manufacturing firms must be able to export as much as they want to import, and arrange their own foreign exchange from external resources.

A market with government policies and regulations such as high tariffs, heavy quotas and other barriers restricting imports is not suitable for an exporting entry mode. Cultural values, language and ways of life affect the choice mainly if striking differences exist between the foreign market and the domestic country. In such cases, non-equity entry modes, such as licensing, which limit the company's commitment in the market, are favoured.

Internal factors

Product, resource and commitment factors also influence a firm's choice regarding establishment of foreign presence.

1 Product factors Highly differentiated products can be priced rather freely yet still remain competitive in the market despite high unit transportation costs and import duties. In such cases, an export strategy is favoured. Volvo in Thailand, for example, has been positioned as an expensive car, priced at more than 1 million baht. This premium price is used to promote a sense of prestige and status to the consumer. Poorly differentiated products must compete on a price basis, which pushes companies towards some form of local production. Technology-intensive products give companies an option to license technology in the foreign market rather than use alternative entry modes.

2 Resource/commitment factors A company's entry mode options increase as its resources in management, capital, technology, production and marketing skills become more abundant. In contrast, the company with limited resources is constrained to use entry modes requiring a relatively small resource commitment.

Changes in internal factors, particularly growing commitment to foreign markets, are the principal forces shaping a company's international evolution. However, the choice of entry mode is directly influenced by the external factors. Moreover, changes in external factors can force the company to revise its entry mode. For example, a restriction on imports of a certain product may force the foreign firm to establish a production facility in the foreign country.

Internationalization strategies

Seven principal strategies can be considered by firms venturing into international business:

1 Indirect exporting

When a firm becomes involved in international business for the first time, many anxieties exist concerning the firm's ability to compete in foreign markets. Indirect channels can be an appropriate form of participation in international business in order to minimize risks and overcome these fears. By using indirect channels a firm can start exporting with no incremental investment in capital, few risks and low start-up costs. Such participation can be considered as part of a developmental process that takes the firm towards more and more international sophistication and commitment.

The indirect exporting approach (i.e. exporting through domestic intermediaries) places the burden of responsibility for sales contacts, negotiations and product delivery on the intermediary within the firm's home market. Indirect channels are less expensive in the early stages of exporting because the cost of foreign market penetration is born directly by the intermediary. However, consider the 'opportunity cost'. Since the intermediary has control over final pricing, a loss of profits may result. Also, the firm's reputation in the marketplace is reflected in the reputation of the intermediary.

Export Management Companies (EMCs) or Export Trading Companies (ETCs) are independent firms contracted by manufacturers to develop export sales, handle shipping and delivery, arrange for payment, and sell products along with other allied, but non-competitive, product lines. The principal advantage of using an indirect export channel is to have access to foreign markets by 'plugging in' to the EMC's foreign market network. This advantage can be strengthened by carefully selecting the EMC/ETC and then supporting it. Support involves working with the

EMC/ETC in formulating a foreign marketing plan for the firm's product line, contributing product information, advertising and technical assistance, and backing up its export operations with prompt servicing of orders.

The primary disadvantage of relying on export intermediaries is the firm's loss of control over foreign sales. This loss can be moderated by specifying in the contract that the manufacturer's approval is required in key decisions and by working intimately with the EMC/ETC. Indirect exporting requires little, if any, foreign market knowledge on the part of the manufacturer and, for the same reason, it isolates the manufacturer from foreign markets.

2 Direct exporting

Direct exporting – exporting through overseas intermediaries – offers several advantages to the manufacturer:

- Partial or full control over the foreign marketing plan.
- Concentrated effort towards marketing the manufacturer's product line.
- Quicker information feedback from the target market.
- Better protection of trademarks, patents, and goodwill.

Direct exporting requires manufacturer familiarity with the procedures of export shipping and international payments. There is a dual problem of developing distribution channel strategies and finding, motivating and supporting overseas distributors in direct exporting. Start-up costs are higher, due to greater information requirements and higher risks.

Direct exporting offers potentially greater profits and challenges. Just as with indirect exporting, there are many available options. The basic criterion is control – the amount of authority you choose to delegate to the foreign partner, which is dictated partially by the basic characteristics and technical sophistication of the product and the need for after-sale service. This situation has a set of criteria different from that of the manufacturer who is exporting a highly technical product requiring after-sale servicing.

3 Licensing/technology transfer/franchising

Licensing

Licensing entails a variety of contractual agreements between the domestic firm (liscensor) and foreign company (liscensee) whereby the domestic firm makes intangible assets such as patents, trade secrets, knowledge, trademarks and company name available to a foreign firm in return for royalties and/or other forms of payments.

When a firm licenses to an independent foreign firm the main purpose is to penetrate a foreign market. Licensing offers both advantages and disadvantages to the Western firm. Some advantages are:

- Licensing is a quick and easy mode to enter foreign markets and requires little capital.
- Royalties received are guaranteed and periodic, whereas exports and direct investment imply fluctuating income and higher risks.
- Western firms can benefit from product development abroad without research expense through technical feedback arrangements.
- Licensing is especially attractive as a low-commitment entry mode, i.e. when a small firm is unable or unwilling to commit resources (managerial, technical, financial) to a foreign market.
- In some countries licensing may be the only way to tap into the market.
- High transportation costs can be overcome by licensing.

Some disadvantages are:

- Unless the licensor possesses distinctive technology, trademark, or a company name that is attractive to potential foreign users, licensing is not the best entry mode to use.
- The licensor lacks control over the marketing plan and production processes in the target market. Today's licensee may become tomorrow's competitors.
- Though royalties are guaranteed and periodic, the absolute size of licensing income can be very small as compared to exporting to or investing in the target market.
- A licensing agreement usually gives exclusive rights of the technology and trademark to the licensee's country. The licensor cannot use an alternative entry mode until the agreement expires.

Technology transfer
The international transfer of technology is made through various

situation-oriented, non-exclusive vehicles. Technology and services expertise can be exchanged through standard export arrangements or project work, licensing agreements, joint ventures and direct investments. Three fundamental considerations must be combined to determine the financial, legal and technological character of any transfer transaction:

• The seller's business plan, financial considerations and company goals.
• The nature of technology/service.
• The objective, business situation, financial and legal environment of the recipient.

The nature of technology/service is the core consideration of technology transfers. Price, method of transfer, terms of exchange, and buyer–seller relationships all revolve around this centre. The price of a service/technology is usually based on the cost of its development.

A company with a unique product or service can sell that product or service at whatever price the market will bear. A service centered on common knowledge will not be able to charge the same price. A technology/service may be based on a patent, trademark right, company know-how and trade secrets. Even if a Western firm is employing a standard manufacturing process, a potential customer may approach the firm to purchase trademark rights which are essential to the success of the end-product.

Franchising

Franchising is a form of licensing in which a company licenses a business system as well as other property rights to an independent company or person. The franchisee operates under the franchisor's trade name and follows policies and procedures laid down by the franchisor. In return, the franchisor receives fees, running royalties and other compensation from the franchisee. This type of entry mode has its advantages and disadvantages. The principal advantages are:

• Rapid expansion into a foreign market with low capital outlays.
• Marketing is standardized and there is a distinctive image.
• The franchisee is highly motivated.
• Political risks are low.

The key disadvantages are:

- Lack of full control over the franchisee's operations.
- Limitations on the franchisor's profit.
- Restrictions imposed by governments on the terms of franchise agreements.

Franchising is particularly attractive when a company has a product that cannot be exported to a foreign target country; does not wish to invest in that country; and has a production process that is easily transferable to an independent party.

Franchising will not work unless the franchisor continuously supports the franchisee. Such support includes supplying equipment, tools, training and finance and general management assistance. The steps to establish franchising systems abroad resemble those of traditional licensing:

- Assessing sales potential in the target market.
- Finding suitable franchising candidates.
- Negotiating the franchise agreement.
- Building a working partnership with the franchisee.

Benetton has achieved its retail distribution through an unusual arrangement with 'agents' in Italy and other European countries. According to one of the company's marketing executives, the term 'franchising' in describing Benetton is a misnomer. Agents of the company are assigned vast territories, largely through verbal agreements, in which they try to develop Benetton retail outlets. They find smaller investors and store operators exhibiting a 'Benetton mentality' to form individual partnerships. An individual agent might supervise and hold an interest in a number of stores.

In 1982, Benetton conducted business with thirty-five agents. Store owners are not required to pay Benetton a fee or a royalty for using its name. They are required to carry only Benetton merchandise, maintain a minimum sales level (equivalent to orders for about 3,500 garments per year), adhere to suggested mark-ups of about 80 per cent above cost, and pay for their orders within ninety days.

4 Contract manufacturing and turnkey projects

Contract manufacturing
Contract manufacturing is a cross between licensing and investment

participation. In contract manufacturing, a host company secures a product or manufacturing process from a Western manufacturer and produces under contract for the Western firm. The production can then be exported or marketed locally.

Contract manufacturing requires a small commitment and financial and management resources. It allows for quick entry into the target country and avoids local ownership problems. It is attractive especially when the target market is too small to justify investment entry, and export entry is too costly. However, it may be difficult or impossible to find a suitable local manufacturer. If a manufacturer is found, substantial technical assistance may be required to improve quality and production levels. There is a risk that the firm may be creating a future competitor.

Turnkey projects

These projects involve a contract for constructing operating facilities that are to be transferred to the foreign owner when ready to commence operations. The contractor is obliged to provide services such as management and worker training after the construction is complete in order to prepare the owner to operate the facilities.

The size and comprehensive nature of these projects sets this type of business apart from most other forms of participation. The majority of these projects are 'mega' projects involving hundreds of millions of dollars. Due to the huge financial commitments required, this kind of business activity is limited to a handful of large firms.

More and more frequently, machinery, equipment, technology and know-how to handle the same technology are sold as a package in the form of complete industrial plants and factories. Sales to Third World countries with limited local construction and engineering capabilities are very often of this form (Ghauri 1983).

There are several reasons why developing countries prefer turnkey projects to direct investment and joint ventures with Western firms. Feelings of distrust and dissatisfaction with Western firms have made economic nationalism a major issue during the past few decades. These feelings continue to worsen for some of the following reasons:

• Most Third World countries are now politically independent and greatly concerned about becoming self-sufficient in the industrial sector.

- Superior know-how and muscle of multinational corporations (MNCs) discourage the development of local industries in the Third World.
- MNCs have been claimed to be responsible for political disturbances in certain countries.
- The results of 'technical assistance' by Western firms have been disappointing in many cases, as poverty and underdevelopment still prevail in many Third World countries.
- There can be advantages in buying an integrated package. It is frequently better for the buyer to deal with just one responsible seller rather than with different sellers who in case of difficulties can blame each other.

Apart from the fact that in some cases turnkey projects are the only way to enter a certain market/country, there may be other advantages for Western firms:

- They do not face the constant threat of nationalization or of increasing restriction by host governments.
- They do not incur any commercial risk while entering a new market.
- They can use turnkey projects as a strategy to charge premium prices for their components.
- They can improve their competitive position as compared to their rivals who sell components. Once they have entered the market through turnkey projects, they can sell the spare parts and components.

5 *Management contracts*

An international management contract gives a Western company the right to manage the day-to-day operations of an enterprise in a foreign market. However, management control is limited to ongoing operations. Management contracts are used mainly to supplement an actual or intended joint venture agreement or a turnkey project.

From an entry strategy perspective, management contracts are unsatisfactory because they do not allow a company to build a permanent market position for its products. Other disadvantages include time-consuming negotiations and the commitment of scarce management talent.

Management contracts are, however, considered a feasible alternative to foreign investments. Transnational firms are not philanthropic organizations, nor do they have any interest in the political or economic goals of local Third World leaders. They are profit-seeking organizations and their decisions are based upon the firms' goals. All alternative routes which are commercially justified are feasible.

6 Foreign production and marketing (direct investment)

Basically, foreign direct investment (FDI) involves the transfer of an entire enterprise to a target market, which enables a company to benefit from its competitive advantages in that market.

Local production may lower costs compared to export entry because of savings in transportation and customs duties and/or lower manufacturing costs resulting from less expensive local inputs of labour, raw material and energy. Such an investment may enable manufacturers to obtain a higher or more uniform quality of supply in the host country.

Direct investment can create marketing advantages such as easier adaptation of products to local preferences and purchasing power. Resources devoted to marketing usually increase, because in this case the manufacturer has more to lose from market failure than with direct exporting or licensing. However, direct investment requires substantially more capital, management, and other company resources, which means bearing more risks – especially political risks. Whenever possible, a company should gain experience in a target country (through exports) before opting for direct investment. Such an investment project must be analysed in the context of its political, legal, economic, social and cultural environments. The many features of a target country's investment climate that need to be assessed by managers are shown in Table 2.1.

From 1950 to 1970, Timex Corporation expanded to a dominant position in the worldwide wristwatch industry with an inexpensive pin-lever watch developed for mass production and assembly. The company's sales were limited to jewellery stores. To break that tradition, Timex introduced its product in various retail outlets, such as drugstores, hardware stores and large merchants. Timex

Table 2.1 Assessing the investment climate of a foreign target country

General political stability
  • Past political behavior
  • Form of government
  • Political, social, ethnic and other conflicts
  • Strength of government

Government policies toward foreign investment
  • Past experience of foreign investors
  • Attitude toward foreign investment
  • Local content requirements
  • Restrictions on foreign ownership
  • Restrictions for foreign staff
  • Incentives for foreign investment
  • Taxation
  • Patent/trademark protection

Macroeconomic environment
  • Role of government in the economy
  • Government development plans/programmes
  • Size/growth rate of population
  • Size/growth rate of gross national product
  • Inflation rate
  • Infrastructure
  • Government economic policies
  • Management–labour reltions
  • Availability of local capital

International payments
  • Balance of payments
  • Foreign exchange position
  • Exchange rate behaviour

built a worldwide network of more than fifteen manufacturing and assembly plants to support sales. These facilities were designed to fabricate piece parts at lowest costs. The lightweight watch movements, cases and straps were shipped by air freight for sub-assembly and final assembly, which optimized the advantages of import duties and tariff regulations.

A foreign direct investment may be made by acquiring an existing operation or by constructing new facilities. A potential investor may look for acquisitions if he finds it difficult to transfer resources or acquire resources locally. An acquisition may give the investor a faster start in developing the foreign target market, because he will have a running enterprise with existing products and markets. By contrast, it can take three to five years for an investor to achieve the same degree of development if he starts from the beginning. An acquisition promises a shorter payback period by creating immediate income for the investor.

Another possible advantage is that new product lines can be acquired. However, this can turn into a disadvantage if the investor has no experience in the new product lines. Thus, while acquisition may have the aforementioned advantages, a potential investor will not necessarily be able to gain them.

Foreign investments are made frequently where there is little or no competition and, hence, it may be difficult to locate a company to buy. The process of fitting the acquired company into current operations and policies can constrain performance and earnings. Substantial problems may be created for the investor, personnel and labour relations may be difficult to change, badwill rather than goodwill may be accrued to existing brands, and facilities may be inefficient and poorly located in relation to future potential markets.

International business executives are also cautioned about difficulties of transferring locally earned funds to the home country – the problem of blocked currency. A US company, H. B. Fuller Co., doing business in Nicaragua is finding it harder to buy raw materials because Nicaragua's central bank is cutting off its supply of hard currency. The same situation was faced by several foreign companies in Mexico and during the last years of President Marcos in the Philippines.

Companies usually prefer to own 100 per cent of their foreign operations in order to secure control and to prevent the dilution of profits. However, sharing ownership is widespread because the Third World countries want local participation and rapid foreign expansion has necessitated bringing in outside resources.

Joint ventures are a special type of ownership-sharing in which equity is owned by two or more companies. Joint ventures are a common form of participation for firms moving beyond the exporting stage to a more regular overseas involvement where local participation may be deemed desirable. Depending on the equity share of the Western company, they may be classified as a majority, minority or 50–50 venture. Joint ventures in many cases may be the only feasible form of investment participation in those countries where sole ventures are either prohibited or discouraged.

Joint ventures provide domestic and Western businesses with a mutually beneficial opportunity to join forces. For both parties, ventures are a means to share both capital and risk and make use of each other's strengths. Problems may arise in these ventures, as there may be more than one party involved in the decision-making process. Joint ventures can be managed successfully with the patience and flexibility of both partners. Usually, however, one of the partners must play the dominant role to steer the business to success.

The most critical decision in a joint venture is the choice of a local partner. For that reason, joint ventures are often compared to marriages. Likewise, joint ventures frequently end in divorce when one or both partners conclude that they can benefit by breaking their relationship.

Each partner enters a joint venture to gain the skills and resources possessed by the other partner. The contribution of the Western company to a joint venture depends on both its own capabilities and those of the local partner as well as on the joint venture's purpose and scope. Usually, the key contribution of the Western partner consists of technology and products while that of the local partner pertains to the knowledge and skills to manage the operation.

7 Countertrade

Countertrade is an ancient form of trading which is emerging anew in world commerce. It refers to a transaction which is characterized by a linkage between exporters and importers of goods or services, in addition to or in place of financial settlements. In ancient times, countertrade took place in the form of barter, where goods of approximately the same value were exchanged without any money being involved. Naturally, these transactions took place at a time when money as a common medium of exchange was not available.

This kind of trade has re-emerged at different times. During the Second World War, American cigarettes were an acceptable medium of exchange in most European countries. Countertrade has appeared in circumstances in which it is more efficient to exchange goods directly than to utilize money as an intermediary. The situations leading to this can be lack of money or lack of appropriate exchange rates.

In the past, countertrade or barter was confined to Eastern bloc countries, because their currencies were not acceptable elsewhere or because they did not have access to foreign exchange. However, recently the use of countertrade has steadily increased. In 1972 countertrade was used by fifteen countries and was commonly referred to only in the context of East–West trade. By 1979 twenty-seven countries were conducting countertrade transactions. By 1983 eighty-eight countries, mostly developing nations, were involved (Bussard 1984).

One primary reason for this development is that the world debt crisis has made ordinary trade financing very risky. Many Third World countries cannot obtain individual trade credits to pay for desired imports. Heavily indebted countries resort to countertrade in order to maintain some trickle of product inflow. Other countries are pursuing bilateralism – they want to sell goods to those countries from whom they import (for example, the Soviet Union's trade with India).

Countertrade is considered an excellent tool to gain entry into a new market in cases where producers feel that marketing is not their strength or where the products face strong international competition. A firm can establish long-term relationships, as the parties are tied down by an agreement. This kind of stability is very valuable, as it reduces demand variations and allows for better planning and efficiency.

Under traditional barter trade, goods are exchanged with goods – for example, cars for toys, sugar for bananas, or machinery for agricultural products. However, now a sophisticated version of countertrade, known as counterpurchase, is emerging. In such an agreement, parties sign two separate contracts specifying the goods and services exchanged. If the exchange is not of equal value partial payment is made in cash.

In another form of countertrade the Western company agrees to supply technology and equipment and receives payment in the form of goods produced by the same plant until final payment is made for the technology. This is known as a 'buyback' agreement.

Another form of countertrade is 'offset'. This is often found in defence-related sectors, and in sales of high-priced items such as aircraft. A developing country purchasing aircraft from France requires certain portions of the aircraft produced and assembled in the purchasing country. Such conditions are placed very commonly on defence and other large-scale contracts and can take many forms, such as co-production, licensing, sub-contracting and joint ventures.

Another form of countertrade is related to clearing. This involves the establishment of clearing accounts to hold deposits and to effect withdrawals for trade. Countries buy and sell different goods and services with the goal of restoring a balanced account in the long term. This is common among the Eastern bloc countries.

Several studies reveal that a shift is occurring from using countertrade reactively to using it proactively, as a new tool for financing and marketing internationally. Another conclusion is that countertrade is here to stay for the foreseeable future, and that Western companies should be prepared to participate in such a non-traditional form of trade.

The increasing importance of countertrade has resulted in the emergence of new specialists (countertrade brokers) who offer to handle such transactions. There are a number of trading houses working internationally, acting frequently as third-party inter-mediaries. Due to their widespread contacts around the world, they can dispose of unwanted countertrade goods much more easily than any individual company. Brokers are more capable of evaluating the risks of such transactions and companies can benefit from their advice while entering into countertrade.

The promise of developing country markets

Third World countries have become increasingly attractive to businesses in recent years. In spite of political instability in some of these countries, which introduces a further risk, they look rather promising. Thailand, for example, has experienced a return to steady economic growth in spite of political in-fighting and some bureaucratic delays resulting from tough economic problems. The growth of the Thai economy is due to the expansion of exports which has led to significant and sustained improvements in the nation's trade balance. Thailand is attempting to achieve the status of a 'Thai style NIC' (Newly Industrialised Country) relying mostly on resource-based and agro-industrial development to take advantage of the country's natural resources. Thailand has become a very attractive location for Japanese offshore production due to its close links to the dollar. Some outstanding Japanese companies such as Sony, Sharp, and Mitsubishi have recently made investments there. A careful analysis of the investment climate in Third World countries may reveal some very profitable opportunities.

(Dohrs 1987:20–2)

There are several reasons why trade with the Third World is being overlooked by scholars and marketers. First, market potential in individual countries is considered too small for targeted marketing efforts. Second, selling costs as a proportion of sales are considerably higher in the Third World. Third, these countries tend to have unstable market structures, making demand estimation difficult. This may discourage export managers who need to make long-term plans for production and sales. Fourth, most non-commodity type imports of the Third World are job orders, requiring special planning and customized production. This requires careful planning and manufacturing by exporters – a requirement many believe is not worth the effort. Fifth, the process of reaching agreements with Third World customers is cumbersome and lengthy, increasing not only the cost of sales but also the commercial risks. Often a business deal fails because of change in administration, import policies or personnel. And sixth, there is a lack of information about market potential and the appropriate strategies to be followed in the Third World.

The purpose of this chapter is to examine the potential of Third World markets and to suggest some appropriate marketing approaches from the perspective of Western firms.

The significance of Third World markets in world trade

While the individual Third World markets may seem too small for concentrated marketing efforts, the Third World collectively constitutes a large proportion of world market potential. More than 70 per cent of the world's population lives in these markets, with the Third World's share in world trade constantly increasing (see Tables 3.1 and 3.2).

Export-oriented growth strategies of some countries, such as Brazil, Taiwan, Singapore and Turkey, have enabled them to play a more active role in world trade. The liberalization of monetary economies by a number of countries in the Third World has led to an increased flow of imported finished and semi-finished goods from Western countries. One of the reasons for these increased imports is that manufacturing industries in these countries are largely dependent on imports. Exports to developing countries account for one-third of total merchandise exports from the USA.

Manufacturing has grown at an impressive pace in most Third World countries. Once primarily agricultural and dependent, these nations are taking on the look of developed economies in terms of the proportion of their gross domestic product (GDP) devoted to industry and services. The countries classified by the World Bank as 'lower-middle income', such as Kenya, Senegal, Bolivia, and Jordan, now average 35 per cent of their GDP from industry and 43 per cent from service, while the share of agriculture has fallen to 22 per cent. Even in the poorest economies, such as those of Bangladesh, Sudan and Mozambique, manufacturing and services

Table 3.1 Shares of production and exports of manufactures by country group, 1965, 1973, and 1985 (per cent)

Country group	Share in production			Share in exports		
	1965	1973	1985	1965	1973	1985
Industrial market economies	85.4	83.9	81.6	92.5	90.0	82.3
Developing countries	14.5	16.0	18.1	7.3	9.9	17.4
Low-income	7.5	7.0	6.9	2.3	1.8	2.1
Middle-income	7.0	9.0	11.2	5.0	8.1	15.3
High-income oil exporters	0.1	0.1	0.3	0.2	0.1	0.3
Total	100.0	100.0	100.0	100.0	100.0	100.0

Source: World Development Report 1987, Washington D.C.: IBRD/World Bank

Table 3.2 Growth in production and exports of manufactures by country group, 1965–73, 1973–85 and 1965–85 (per cent)

Country group	Growth in production			Growth in exports		
	1965–73	1973–85	1965–85	1965–73	1973–85	1965–85
Industrial market economies	5.3	3.0	3.8	10.6	4.4	6.8
Developing countries	9.0	6.0	7.2	11.6	12.3	12.2
Low-income	8.9	7.9	7.5	2.4	8.7	6.0
Middle-income	9.1	5.0	6.6	14.9	12.9	13.8
High-income oil exporters	10.6	7.5[a]	8.4[a]	16.2	11.5	16.0
Total	5.8	3.5	4.5	10.7	5.3	7.4

Source: World Development Report 1987, Washington D.C.: IBRD/World Bank

Note: a. End period is 1984 instead of 1985.

account for 55 per cent of GDP, while the share of agriculture has fallen from 48 per cent to 35 per cent (Kindel and Tietelman 1983).

These changes, plus a large and increasing GDP, provide opportunities for products tailored to the needs of the Third World. Western firms manufacturing machine tools and instruments are realizing the great potential of these markets. Pharmaceutical firms such as Sterling, Ciba–Geigy, Pfizer and Astra are reaping substantial profits from selling vaccines and medicines which can be shipped to faraway markets and which can be stored without refrigeration. Aircraft manufacturers are working on aircraft designed specifically for developing nations. Lockheed Aircraft, whose Hercules turboprop is a popular aircraft in the Third World, has developed several prototypes for transport planes that can carry bulk commodities at relatively low cost. Opportunities are available to be successful in a large market – if Western firms apply sound marketing principles.

The problem in implementing an export strategy is that in trying to increase their exports most Third World countries are forced to increase their imports of technology, manufactured parts and semi-finished goods. Usually, at least some of the foreign exchange obtained through higher exports is expended on imports of consumer products. Increasing consumer expectations and converging lifestyles in these countries have led to higher imports and consumption of many products once available only to consumers in industrialized countries.

Some characteristics of Third World markets

It may be helpful to review the economic and marketing characteristics of Third World countries before discussing their marketing implications. For this purpose, Third World nations are classified into three relatively homogeneous groups based on demographic and economic commonalities (see Table 3.3).

The ability of most Third World nations to engage in international business is severely constrained by how much they owe to other nations. Useful information on indebtedness, according to four risk groups, based on the countries debt service requirements is shown in Table 3.4. These risk classifications influence countries' ability to borrow from international banks.

Some macroeconomic characteristics of the Third World are relevant to successful marketing. Most Western companies are

Table 3.3 A market-oriented classification of Third World countries

Classification examples	Demographic make-up	Marketing implications
DEPENDENT Most countries in Africa, Asia and a few in South America (e.g., Bolivia, Honduras)	Population growth: 3% Median age: 16 Children: 5+ Infant mortality: 100 per 1,000 births Life expectancy: 40 years	Demand goods and services related to food, clothing, housing, education and medical care. Investments related to extractive activities (agriculture and mining) are undertaken. Government/State Economic Enterprises are the major buying groups.
SEEKERS Most of Latin America, some in Asia (Malaysia, Indonesia, Philippines) and some in Africa (Morocco, Tunisia, Egypt, Algeria)	Population growth: 1.5 to 2.5% Median age: 20 Children: 4+ Infant mortality: 50 to 100 per 1,000 births Life expectancy: 60 years	Infrastructure-related projects are high priority (construction equipment, machinery, chemicals and so on). Good opportunities for technology sales and turnkey projects. Independent trading groups and a few large holding companies have much influence.
CLIMBERS Brazil, Greece, Hong Kong, Israel, Portugal, Spain, Taiwan, Turkey, South Korea	Children: 2 to 3 Median age: Higher than 20	Industrialization and service sector expenditures assume greater importance. Private enterprises have become more dominant than state agencies. Good opportunities for joint ventures and technology agreements. Export-intensive projects are top priority.

Source: Adapted from Cavusgil 1985:576–99

Table 3.4 The Third World's ability to meet debt-service requirements*

Relative standing	1985 ranking	1989 ranking
Good	Malaysia ($1.5) Taiwan	Ivory Coast ($0.7) Malaysia ($2.5) Taiwan Thailand ($1.3)
Fair	Columbia ($1.4) Indonesia ($3.6) Ivory Coast ($1) S. Korea ($4.6) Thailand ($1.2) Tunisia ($0.7) Venezuela ($3.9)	Algeria ($1.7) Columbia ($2) Ecuador ($1.3) Indonesia ($4.7) S. Korea ($4.4) Tunisia ($0.6) Turkey ($2.8) Venezuela ($2.1)
Poor	Algeria ($4.5) Brazil ($14.9) Ecuador ($1.8) Philippines ($2) Turkey ($3.2)	Brazil ($15.9) Chile ($2.6) Egypt ($1.5) Philippines ($2)
High risk	Argentina ($5) Bolivia ($0.5) Chile ($1.9) Egypt ($2.6) Mexico ($17.9) Morocco ($2.1) Nigeria ($4.3) Peru ($2.3) Uruguay ($0.8)	Argentina ($3.9) Bolivia ($0.3) Mexico ($14.1) Morocco ($1.6) Nigeria ($2.2) Peru ($1.9) Uruguay ($0.5)

Source: *Business International*, 20 December 1985: 407
Note: * Rankings are based on estimates of debt-service ratios (projected debt service divided by exports of goods and services in US$ terms). Figures in parentheses reflect World Bank projections of debt service on long term public and publicity guaranteed debt for the year in question in US$ billions.

accustomed to marketing in a buyer's market – i.e., a market with numerous buyers. Domestic markets in the Third World are characterized by:

- A seller's market, where individual customer concerns are not crucial in consumer goods.
- A concentrated market, where most personal selling strategies require modification.

Many Third World countries are liberalizing their economies, although many are still far from becoming market economies. This is due to various reasons. First, domestic markets are small in terms of absolute size and purchasing power. This leads to natural monopolies, where the production or imports of a single entrepreneur become more efficient than several entrepreneurs. Even with the absence of export restrictions, competition for a share of domestic market is accompanied by a relatively low return, thereby discouraging new entries.

Second, wholesale distribution in many of the Third World countries is controlled by manufacturers or importers, thus creating a formidable barrier to entry. New entrants soon discover that, although their products may be a better buy, there is no way of distributing the product through existing channels. Wholesalers tend to control the retail outlets in terms of their product portfolios and financing agreements. These wholesalers can dictate the product mix to the retailers in the absence of fair-trade regulations and anti-trust laws. These market imperfections result in highly controlled markets in which the buyer must purchase whatever is offered. The power of natural monopolies remains unchallenged in most cases because of their traditional ties to the government and each other.

Third World markets are extremely concentrated in decision-making and market potential. Government involvement is more than regulatory. The active economic role played by governments in the Third World is evident in the ability of the private sector to accumulate capital required for certain investments, in national and economic security issues, and in subsidizing a sector.

The share of state-owned economic enterprises (SEEs) in most Third World economies is quite substantial, although privatization of government-controlled enterprises is underway in most developing countries. In Brazil the government still controls more than 75 per cent of postal services, telecommunications, electricity, gas, railways, oil production, coal and steel industries. Banking, shipping and airlines, in addition to the above-mentioned industries, are controlled by the state in India and Pakistan. The same pattern occurs in Mexico. In Turkey, SEEs control more than 55 per cent of the manufacturing industry, ranging from textiles and ceramics to steel.

Active participation of the government sector in economic activity can often be explained by ambitious development goals and historical factors. The government is involved indirectly through centralized economic planning, in addition to being involved

directly in the economy through ownership of economic enterprises. Government intervention increases concentration in these
economies in the sense that business deals are not made with
individual buyers, but with bureaucrats in various government
agencies. It is a common practice for international marketers to
start sales calls with civil servants at the capital city instead of with
the actual buyer. Like the old adage, 'All roads lead to Rome', all
deals in the Third World go through the government at one point or
another.

Geographical concentration is a reality. For the private sector, 50
per cent of manufacturing occurs in only three of sixty-seven
provinces in Turkey. More than one-fifth of the 50 million people in
Egypt live in or around Cairo. A direct implication of these
observations is that the task of identifying target buyers and
assessing competition is made easier.

Phases in the marketing process

It is helpful to conceptualize the marketing process to Third World
countries in six phases (see Figure 3.1). The process is typical of the
experience encountered by a Western firm selling to private and
government sectors in developing countries. It is more descriptive
of the unusual, rather than routine, major purchases made by the
Third World (Ghauri 1983, Jansson 1986).

Phase one: scanning

Marketing to Third World countries begins with the identification
of new opportunities. Most aggressive firms develop sophisticated
market intelligence systems to monitor worldwide sales opportunities on a continuous basis. Information from a variety of sources
is sought and evaluated. Internally, travelling managers, subsidiaries and overseas representatives feed information to a central office.
Externally, useful information about new opportunities may be
gathered from the Agency for International Development, the
World Bank, foreign embassies, international banks, industrial
organizations and other firms. Many publications, such as the bi-
monthly periodical *Worldwide Projects*, are also helpful.

Although most of the Third World is made up of non-socialist

Phase 1
SCANNING

Market surveillance to
learn about forthcoming
projects

Phase 2
THE APPROACH

Presentation of critical information
to buyer in order to increase awareness
and to influence writing of technical
specifications

Phase 3
COMPETITIVE BIDDING

Preparation and submission
of bid

Phase 4
NEGOTIATIONS

Technical and economic evaluation
of bid; informal and formal meetings
concluding in a final bidding

Phase 5
COMPLETION

Carrying out the project activity, typically
involving construction, training and service

Phase 6
FOLLOW-UP

Monitoring project performance and
cultivating 'spin-off' sales

Figure 3.1 The process of marketing to developing countries

countries, buyers from these countries must still comply with an
annual economic plan or, for example, the yearly implementation
of a five-year development plan. These plans differ in detail and
directiveness from country to country. Nevertheless, most plans are
substantially directive, although they may be called 'advisory' for
political reasons.

Understanding the process of plan preparation and becoming
familiar with the plan itself is the first step in successful marketing
to the Third World. It is through the planning process that most

Third World governments announce their import priorities and investment plans. English texts of annual plans are usually available.

Industrial–sectorial programmes are usually integral parts of development plans. These are important documents for marketing planning. Note that in many nations, plans change with governments. Thus, the international marketer must be familiar with the programmes of political parties. That is where policy guidelines for annual plans can be found.

The situation is not much different for sectors that are outside the scope of annual plans or where plans are not directive. Almost all private and government enterprises are forced to operate with high financial leverages, given the insufficient capital accumulation in these countries. Most financing originates from private/state-owned banks and direct–indirect government subsidies. Government subsidies, such as tax rebates and low-interest credits, are more directive than the plan in most cases. It is almost impossible to realize an investment in many of the Third World countries without such incentives. Therefore, government interference and control is quite dramatic even in those sectors that appear not to be regulated by plans.

Western marketers also stay abreast of sales opportunities through their overseas representatives/agents, especially in major markets. These representatives are local business people who ordinarily work on a commission-on-sales basis. They are familiar with the realities of the market and are in a position to evaluate the plans and programmes efficiently, and identify sales opportunities. In addition to monitoring the market they provide valuable assistance in lengthy sales negotiations.

There are two types of representative: exclusive and non-exclusive. Exclusive representatives are the only representatives for a company in a country. They are compensated whether or not they have anything to do with the sales. Experience shows that in concentrated and relatively small markets, obtaining a non-exclusive representative may be counterproductive.

Several considerations are relevant to selecting an exclusive representative. First, exclusive representatives may attempt to represent more than one company. The international marketer should be careful in selecting representatives to ensure there is no conflict of interest. An exclusive representative may be an agent for several companies in related businesses in order to secure a certain level of sales commissions.

Second, most representatives have their own businesses and essentially run a 'one-person show'. There is always a majority shareholder, or a family who is known to the locals as the owner, even if there is a professional manager running office operations. The personal history and reputation of this person or family is extremely important. A representative's business is based on reputation and contacts. Therefore, it is always advisable to check on the history and degree of success of the representative with other clients.

Third, corruption is a reality in most Third World countries. The Western marketer would be in a difficult position when confronted with such a sensitive issue without the help and commitment of an exclusive representative.

Phase two: the approach

The marketer must approach the buyer with relevant information and attempt to influence the writing of a tender specification, which usually takes the form of a feasibility report, once the opportunity for a specific project is identified. The marketer's aim is to present information on production and technological capabilities, solvency, and the likelihood of successful completion of the project. This is done to establish familiarity and confidence, and to reduce any perceived risk on the part of the potential buyer.

An important objective of the marketing effort is to achieve a 'first-mover' advantage. A marketer who can pre-empt competitors and be first in supplying relevant information to buyers will have a head start in the selling process. Marketers can tie up prospective buyers through several strategies:

- A technical solution to buyers' problems.
- Social linkages between buyers and sellers.
- Financial linkages in terms of provisions for financing the project.
- Other informational linkages.

These strategies are illustrated in Figure 3.2. In the final analysis, the choice of a supplier boils down to human judgement. Hence, the importance of informal social contacts cannot be overemphasized.

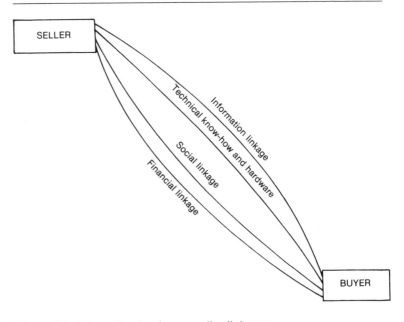

Figure 3.2 Strengthening buyer–seller linkages

Jansson (1986) compares the creation of first-mover advantage to the spinning of a web, in that the buyer is encircled while the competitors are closed out. Growing interdependence between buyers and sellers, strengthened through the four types of linkage, facilitates successful bidding. In the absence of a first-mover advantage marketers should consider carefully any further allocation of time and resources to the particular project. At this point, considerable marketing efforts have already been expended in identifying and cultivating new opportunities. Any additional expenses may be useless if a competitor already has the first-mover advantage.

Consideration of the following issues may be helpful in determining the desirability of any further commitment to the project:

- Can any information be provided to the buyer which would place you in a stronger position?
- What level of previous influence do you have with the buyer?
- Even if the product offerings are comparable, can you offer a more attractive financing option to the buyer?

- Can you gain a competitive edge by using domestic materials or by directing end-products into export markets?
- Is there an opportunity to tie up the buyer in order to supply managerial/technical services and other products once the operation is completed?

A major objective of the first mover is to effect the tender specifications before they are finalized in a feasibility report. The marketer must find out who is responsible for the delineation of tender specifications and, then, supply technical and other information to the buyer's project team. It is not unusual for marketers to assist buyers with various project-related studies at this stage.

There are several reasons why feasibility reports precede the actual solicitation of bids. Often, the buying organizations have to submit a feasibility report to take advantage of various incentives and obtain credit from local international sources. Government generally requires a feasibility report to show compliance to plans and overall economic objectives. Favoured projects include those building infrastructure, improving the balance of payments either by import substitution or by creating export opportunities, creating employment opportunities, having high added value, and/or transferring appropriate technology.

Most feasibility reports are prepared for a specific type of investment with detailed specifications. Although competitive bidding is an accepted practice, many prospective bidders are eliminated because technical specifications are often prepared for a specific group of suppliers. In some cases selection of suppliers precedes the preparation of a feasibility report. This means that sales efforts must begin prior to the preparation of feasibility reports.

A feasibility report is a technical documentation of the proposed project. A considerable amount of expertise and technical knowhow is required to prepare this report. Usually, the managerial expertise can be found locally. The technical expertise, on the other hand, is usually unavailable, and the customary approach is to consult published reports or international consultants. Since many projects are duplicates of similar investments in industrialized economies, visits to overseas sites by the buyer's project team are also common. Potential clients can be invited to tour the marketer's facilities in the home market and elsewhere.

The local exclusive representatives usually lack technical know-how and they may not have the authority to make commitments on behalf of the foreign vendor. When the prospective project warrants, a team must be in direct contact with the potential buyer during the preparation of the feasibility study. One way of accomplishing this is for sellers in the West to have *ad hoc* project teams for Third World markets which can be organized quickly and hence avoid missing potential opportunities.

It is not unusual for an international consulting firm to be assigned to the preparation of the feasibility report for large-scale projects. Usually this is a loan-requirement for large-scale projects financed through international financial markets. However, the use of a consulting firm does not necessarily guarantee a better report, since most international consultants are unfamiliar with the particular market. The firm may overlook major factors or rely upon incomplete information. Furthermore, political and business considerations force international consultants to act as mediators in most cases. Consulting firms will rarely be willing to make radical suggestions, as decisions relating to large investment/import projects may result in power struggles and political controversies in Third World countries.

Phase three: competitive bidding

A tender is published and bids are solicited from all interested vendors once the technical specifications are set. Technical terms and conditions are followed by the so-called 'administrative terms and conditions' (ATC) for large-scale projects. Various legal, financial and administrative issues are spelled out and procurement procedures are revealed.

A critical decision by the international marketer at this stage relates to the amount of time and other resources to be invested in preparing the bid. It is expensive to produce bids, particularly for large projects, but it is hoped that the likelihood of a successful bid has been strengthened by tying up the buyer in the previous stage.

Purchasing by the government or SEE is regulated by law in most Third World countries. This is helpful to the supplier because the organizational buying process and the authority and responsibility of each buying unit is clearly described in such laws. The regulations relating to government procurement state how requisitions are to be placed, who will have decision-making authority, and how the decision will be implemented. The international marketer must become familiar with these regulations. However, it should be noted that governments and SEEs are not always obliged to follow the law. This is true especially for certain clauses specifying the conditions under which a contract can be awarded.

There are no such regulations in privately owned corporations. The organizational structures of these corporations are usually centralized. Occasionally, shares of even the largest corporations are controlled by a few individuals or families. Therefore, the international marketer does not have to look far in identifying key decision-makers.

This identification is often more difficult with government/SEE purchases. International marketers may be surprised to discover that they have to talk to a dozen people from different echelons and divisions of an agency or agencies. Some agency personnel may even pretend to be real decision-makers. A local representative may provide helpful inside information in this regard.

Some international marketers concentrate their efforts on the person who appears to be the final decision-maker and neglect or even avoid others in the process. Due to cultural reasons, this strategy backfires in many Third World countries. Bureaucrats at lower levels of the hierarchy are generally frustrated and alienated because of low pay, underemployment, elitism and other factors. Hence, being bypassed by a foreign supplier may be insulting. A major sales opportunity was lost by a US textile company because of this oversight. An expert in the state planning organization argued that the supplier's technology was inappropriate and convinced the Minister of Finance who was negotiating the financing not to award the contract, even though the Minister of Industry and the general manager of the buying corporation were convinced it was the best offer.

Phase four: negotiations

Submitted bids are evaluated by the buyer from both technical and economic perspectives. Typically, bids are short-listed and some vendors are invited for further discussions, which usually marks the beginning of lengthy negotiations. These meetings provide opportunities for marketers to present additional explanations and details. These can be crucial in terms of their impact on the outcome.

Due to increasing international competition, the Third World drives a hard bargain. Third World buyers may play Western suppliers against each other through bilateral or multilateral agreements. Applying uniform import taxes, pooling commodity imports and cartel-type agreements are common. Pooling import purchases such as fertilizers and tractors for commodity production from multinational corporations is an example of such agreements.

Many Third World countries lack the necessary foreign exchange to finance purchases. Total financing by the seller is a common practice now in large-scale projects. Tight international money markets and the low credit ratings of many Third World countries force them to look for the best payment terms.

Japanese firms are quite successful in competitive bidding because they provide complete financial packages to the Third World. Limitations in certain products/process attributes may be overcome by strengths in financial terms, such as low interest, total financing, long maturity and grace periods. Cooperation with financial institutions becomes a necessary ingredient for most negotiations. Some examples are provided in Chapter Six. At the same time, these countries are engaging increasingly in counter-trade deals, where part of the import is paid for with goods rather than cash. Nearly a hundred countries now require countertrade purchases from their foreign suppliers (Huszagh and Huszagh 1986).

The balance of trade continues to be a serious problem for most Third World countries. Their desire to improve their export situation enhances the seller's bargaining power. A contract for the construction of a vegetable processing plant was granted to a French firm because the technology it offered, although expensive, was capable of producing goods that could be exported to the European community.

Some developing countries are attempting to alter existing economic ties and establish alternative trade channels. The increasing aggressiveness of Eastern Europe in international markets provides additional bargaining power for most Third World countries. Western manufacturers limit Third World buyers' options. A large project involving machine tools was not awarded to a US bidder because it insisted on providing exclusively parts and supplies needed later. In contrast, Japanese bidders included a comparison of alternative sources from a variety of countries.

In certain countries it is necessary to deal with intermediaries close to the government in order to accomplish any business deal. Their commissions (usually about 10 per cent) are paid almost automatically. 'Lubrication' or 'grease payments' are a way of life in most Third World countries even though considered unethical by some. International marketers should be prepared to take positions on such issues and make their positions known from the outset. Although such payments are considered bribes by Western standards, intermediaries believe them to be payments for their services.

Local representatives will be able to advise the international marketer on such matters, and establishing cordial relationships with the negotiating party may help to reduce this expense. Since many cultures mix interpersonal relations with business, a company with established, friendly relations may not have to deal with corruption at all.

The supplier's ability to utilize local resources is an additional feature attractive to most Third World buyers. Sellers who can demonstrate that their offers create additional jobs and added value will have greater bargaining power, particularly with government purchasers.

Note that Third World buyers may not place a high value on quality, especially when imported products are intended for sale within the domestic market. Therefore, emphasizing quality is not likely to increase the seller's bargaining strength in case of a price disadvantage. In many cases, sellers should try to provide similar quality at lower prices. For instance, Italy is the preferred supply source for aluminum die-casting because of its low price. However, the Silesium content of the material is low and the metal is, in fact, recycled and, therefore, tired. Nevertheless, buyers are willing to sacrifice quality for price.

Sellers have a stronger bargaining position in those cases where Third World procurement is related to export-oriented programmes and if any assistance is needed in marketing the final product.

Often Third World countries are unable to market what they produce because they cannot penetrate the international distribution channels. The seller who has some control over such channels or who can secure the cooperation of a trading company or a broker has considerable bargaining power in negotiations. The Sogo Shosha, Japanese general trading companies, have been instrumental in finding markets for Third World products primarily because of their global networks.

Finally, an important element strengthening the seller's bargaining power is the managerial expertise provided in post-investment operations. Many Third World countries are hesitant to acquire turnkey agreements for various reasons.

First, these countries feel they do not have the managerial expertise needed to run the operations successfully. Second, even if the operations can be handled, marketing becomes a problem. Third, and most importantly, Third World buyers feel that they are sold inappropriate or outdated technology. As a solution, turnkey-plus or build-own-and-operate arrangements are favoured by many Third World countries. The supplier guarantees to buy part of the end-products or makes an equity investment in this arrangement. The seller may be asked to provide the managerial expertise needed to run the operation. The developing country partner agrees to buy the seller out after a specific period. In this way, the burden of choosing the right kind of investment is placed on the seller. The seller's risk is greater in such an agreement, but his bargaining position is strengthened. International marketers who are willing to take such risks are better equipped for penetrating Third World markets.

Phase five: completion

Once a certain supplier is selected, delivery, installment, and the initiation of different components take place. Typically, a temporary project organization is formed to complete this assignment. Most projects in Third World countries involve a combination of construction, personnel training, project management and service. The smoothness of the implementation will be critical to the supplier's long-term success. A supplier can experience numerous problems and delays in coping with local subcontractors, local authorities, import regulations, union procedures and other constraints within the local environment. Successful suppliers will be those who expect such problems and take active steps to deal with them.

Table 3.5 Guidelines for marketing to Third World countries

- Follow development plans, yearly programmes, government programmes and programmes of political parties closely. These are easily accessible.

- Become familiar with government incentives for investments. These will determine future demand.

- Select a good exclusive local representative. Make sure that he does not represent competitors, that he has an area of specialization and that he is reliable.

- Become familiar with the process of preparing a feasibility report.

- Provide technical know-how during the preparation of technical specifications.

- Maintain close contact with domestic and international consulting organizations who may be preparing technical specifications or feasibility reports. Keep in touch with local technocrats and engineers. They are small in number and easily accessible. They will determine what will be bought.

- Establish friendly relations with potential buyers even if they are not buying now. It is an inexpensive but very effective public relations effort.

- Become familiar with regulations related to government and State Economic Enterprise procurements. Note that governmental agencies do not have to follow such regulations all of the time.

- Find the 'Lion' in each organization. In each organization one or two people will have the 'final say'. Make sure that you know who they are, but never ignore others who are involved.

- Become familiar with the international agreements of the developing country. Do not use political–military alliances as a part of your sales strategy.

- Offer a complete deal. Be ready to finance your own sales.

- Certain issues prove efficient in negotiating sales. The ability of your offer to improve the balance of payments, create employment, add value, utilize local resources, decrease import dependence, increase the international options of the country both in terms of buying and selling in the future, and improve the flexibility of the operations are examples.

- Be prepared to deal with bribery. Use your local representative and stay out of it.

Phase six: follow-up

Successful completion of a project usually generates a considerable number of spin-off sales. Opportunities exist for selling a service contract, parts and equipment, software and other supplementary products. Hence, it is desirable to maintain contact with the customer; to ensure satisfaction and to learn about developing projects. A company must maintain a reasonable guarantee period in addition to an adequate level of after-sales service for its customers.

Conclusion

Neglected Third World markets are beginning to gain importance in the light of recent pressures to globalize marketing operations. It is a misconception that Third World markets are disorganized and chaotic. On the contrary, the buying process is usually more formalized. The fact that Third World markets are more concentrated and that the government is an integral part of most business operations provides opportunities for the international marketer.

Most buying is performed by organizations, either privately owned or government operated. Markets are basically sellers' markets. Buying organizations follow a formal approach in their purchases. Most purchases are based on a feasibility plan which contains a strong macroeconomic orientation for development. A list of pertinent guidelines is provided in Table 3.5.

Recognize that these suggestions require the seller to assemble a team which includes both managerial and technical experts. An unfortunate mistake made by many companies is sending a sales representative and expecting him to close deals alone. This usually results in the loss of markets. Appropriate marketing strategies promise considerable rewards from Third World markets, given the competitive nature of global markets.

Finally, each Third World country is unique even though there are some common features. Hence, each country's potential must be viewed within the context of its own special characteristics.

Chapter four

A framework for international business negotiations

'A fundamental characteristic of the Chinese negotiating style is the effort to identify a sympathetic counterpart in the foreign team, to cultivate a personal relationship – a sense of friendship – and then to manipulate feelings of goodwill, obligations, guilt or dependence to achieve their negotiating objectives. Friendship to the Chinese way of thinking implies the obligation to provide support and assistance to one's friend.'

The Chinese view negotiations as an effort to reconcile the principles and objectives of the two sides and to test the foreign teams' commitment to a relationship. Chinese do not see negotiation as a highly technical, impersonal process of haggling over details, in which the two sides initially table their maximum position and then seek to move to a point of convergence through incremental compromises.

According to one author, 'To establish a framework for a relationship, it has been my experience that the P.R.C. team will press the U.S. party at the outset to accept certain general principles. These political ground rules will then be used to constrain your bargaining flexibility and to test the sincerity of your desire to develop and sustain a relationship with the Chinese.'

(Ravies 1987:36)

No two Third World countries will exhibit the same negotiation style. It is important to know in advance the country and the culture so that you are better prepared for the negotiation process.

The development of the negotiation process and how the parties perceive the relationship is crucial in traditional business negotiation as well as in project sales negotiations. A model or framework of negotiation has to be dynamic in nature. It is characterized by a group of variables called 'atmosphere' in our world. The atmosphere not only explains the perceptions of the parties but also the progress of the process – i.e., how it develops through different stages. The emphasis in this chapter is on international business negotiations between parties having a problem-solving orientation, not conflict- or game-oriented negotiations.

An overall framework for business negotiations has three groups of variables: background factors, process, and atmosphere (Figure 4.1). It is the negotiation process, not the outcome, that is of primary interest here. The outcome is indicated by wavy lines, while broken lines show feedback from process to background. Since the negotiation process is inherently dynamic, a certain perception of the parties or a particular development in the process may influence a change in the background factors.

Background factors

This group of variables serves as a background to the process. They influence the process of negotiation and atmosphere. The effect of different variables on the process and its different stages varies in intensity. One of these variables may influence one stage positively and another negatively. A positive influence means that the process saves time and continues smoothly, while a negative influence causes delay and hindrances.

In all business relations, parties have objectives when entering into negotiations. Objectives are defined as the end state each party desires to achieve. They are often classified as common, conflicting or complementary. For example, parties have a common interest if both want a successful transaction to take place. At the same time their interests may conflict, since profit to one is cost to the other. In terms of complementary interest, buyers in international deals are concerned with acquiring appropriate technology to build an infrastructure. On the other hand, sellers want to enter a particular market and expect to do future business with it and the surrounding countries' markets.

Common and complementary objectives affect the negotiation process directly and positively, whereas conflicting objectives have negative effects. These effects in turn influence the atmosphere and the outcome. Opportunity for an agreement decreases as conflict-

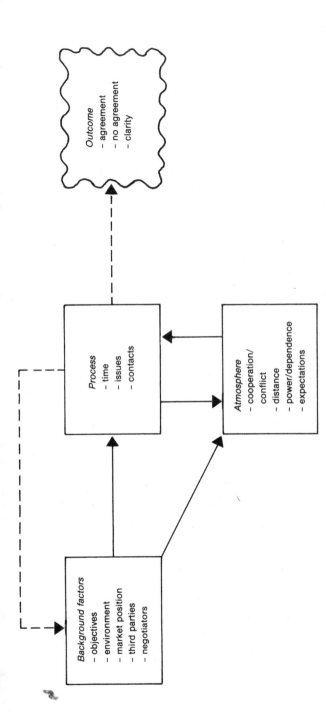

Figure 4.1 An overall framework for business negotiations
Source: Ghauri 1983:46

ing objectives dominate in a relationship; it increases as common and complementary objectives dominate.

The environment refers to the political, social and cultural milieu of the parties. Variation of parties with respect to environment often hinders the negotiation process. There are greater chances of interaction interferences when unfamiliar parties, having different behaviours, interact with one another. Some of the characteristics directly influence the process while others directly influence the atmosphere. Political and social aspects influence the process, and cultural aspects plus the behaviour of the parties influence the atmosphere.

The parties' market position is another background variable influencing the negotiation process. The number of buyers and sellers in the market determines the number of alternatives available to each party, which, in turn, affects the amount of pressure imposed by its counterpart within the market. The process and bargaining position of the buyer or seller can be affected if either one has monopolistic power in the marketplace. For example, if there are a large number of sellers and only one buyer the latter can dominate. Empirical studies reveal that whenever there is a shortage of orders in the market, buyers are in a better bargaining position.

Most international business deals involve third parties – i.e., parties other than the seller and buyer – such as governments, agents, consultants and subcontractors. These parties may influence the negotiation process as they have different objectives. Often, Third World governments are involved and influence the buyers towards complementary objectives, such as infrastructure, employment opportunities, foreign exchange considerations and any other prospective relationship between the two countries. The sellers' agents play an important role since they can help bridge environmental differences and smooth the background for negotiations. Financiers may also be involved as third parties – for example, the World Bank. These financiers influence the negotiation process by demanding different types of guarantees and documents which may delay the process.

Negotiators influence the negotiation process with their own experience and negotiation skills. Empirical studies show that marketing skills in addition to persuasion skills, awareness of environmental factors and a positive behaviour affect the process to a great extent. Even the influence of political affiliations cannot be ignored here. Negotiators operate within two limits: first, they act to increase common interests and to expand cooperation among the parties; second, they act to maximize their own interests and to ensure an agreement valuable for themselves.

The personality of the negotiators may also play a role, particularly when information about each other is lacking and there is greater stress. Case studies indicate that even if negotiators from the seller's side do not have enough information on competitors they can handle the situation effectively due to experience and personality. A good personality is defined as an individual with ability to make others understand his position, to approach strangers with ease and confidence, and to appreciate the other person's position. However, skills of negotiators are related to different objectives and motivations, pertaining to different people and professions. Negotiators with a technical background may place more emphasis on technical issues, while those with a business background might consider other issues to be more important.

Atmosphere

The relationship developed during the negotiation process between the parties is characterized by an atmosphere which is of basic importance to the process as a whole. The atmosphere and the process affect each other through interaction at each stage. Atmosphere is defined as the perceived milieu around the interaction, how the parties perceive each other's behaviour, and the properties of the process. It enhances the dynamics of the process. Some atmosphere characteristics are dominant at one stage; others at another stage. The offer stage is dominated by cooperation rather than conflict, as parties look for technical solutions for buyers. Dominance of various atmosphere characteristics changes from process to process. Perceived distance is more dominant in processes among unfamiliar parties than with parties belonging to the same environment.

The existence of both conflict and cooperation is a fundamental characteristic of the negotiation process. On one hand, parties have some common interests in finding a solution to the problem which fits both the supplier's ability and the user's need. On the other hand, a conflict of interest may arise, as cost to one is income to the other.

The magnitude of conflict or cooperation in the atmosphere

depends upon the objectives of the parties to the negotiation. Some relationships are more complementary – and consequently less conflicting – than others. The degree of conflict or cooperation during different stages of the negotiation process is often a function of what issues are dealt with, while the degree of conflict or cooperation in the atmosphere is a function of how the parties handle various problems. Conflict is sometimes perceived, without the existence of real conflict, due to a misunderstanding of each other's behaviour. The more unfamiliar the parties are with one another, the higher the risk for such perceived conflicts (Ghauri and Johanson 1979).

Distance between parties refers to each party's ability to understand the other's capabilities and needs. It is dependent on differences between the parties and on their business experiences with other countries. Firms which have previously done business with each other are expected to be closer than those which have not. One of the functions of the negotiation process is to reduce or overcome the distance between parties. This is particularly important when doing business with the Third World, where parties are normally unfamiliar with each other. It is not only physical distance but also psychic or mental distance which influences the process of negotiations (Hallen and Wiedersheim-Paul 1979).

The power/dependence relation is another basic characteristic of all negotiation processes. It is closely related to the objective power relation, which is influenced by the value of the relationship to the parties and their available alternatives. Background factors – for example, the market position – can influence the power/dependence relation. The ability to control a relationship is related to the perceived power of two parties, their relative expertise and access to information.

This power is a property of the relationship and not an attribute of the actor. In fact it is closely related to dependence. Therefore, the power relationship is in balance if both parties have equal power. The power relationship is unbalanced if one of the parties has more power, or if one party is dependent on the other (Emerson 1962).

One function of the negotiation process is to bring about some level of conformity in the power/dependence relation perception. If there is a big difference between the two parties' perceptions the negotiation process may be halted and a deal will only be made if this situation is acceptable to both parties.

The last aspect of atmosphere concerns two types of expectations. First, there are long-term expectations regarding the possibilities and values of future deals. The stronger these expectations are, the more inclined the negotiators are to agree on the present deal. Second, there are short-term expectations concerning prospects for the present deal. Long-term expectations are related to primary objectives. The parties' decision to enter negotiations and to continue after each stage implies expectations of a better outcome from participating than from not participating. This compels the parties to proceed from one stage to the next. Expectations develop and change in different stages of the process and can also be related to expectations in organizational problem-solving, as discussed by Cyert and March (1963).

The negotiation process

The negotiation process is often described in terms of its different stages (for example, Kennedy 1985, Kapoor 1970, UNIDO 1975 and Ghauri 1983 and 1986). These stages are:

Offer
Informal meetings
Planning for formal negotiations
Formal negotiations
Implementation

If parties do not agree on all issues at this final stage and still find it useful to continue negotiating, two more stages may take place:

Informal meetings II
Formal negotiations II

A stage of the process refers to a specific time and includes all actions and communications by any party pertaining to negotiations made during that period. Parties communicate with each other to exchange information within each stage. A particular stage ends when parties decide to proceed further into the next stage or decide to abandon the communication if they see no point in further negotiations. In the offer stage, parties attempt to understand each other's needs and demands, and decide either to proceed with the following stage, informal meetings, or, due to incompatibility of each other's demands, not to proceed further, whereupon the negotiations end without agreement.

Some authors (for example, Smith and Wells 1975) have studied the negotiation process in terms of technical, commercial and other issues. The process of negotiation is considered with respect to different stages and issues. Most of these issues are discussed simultaneously, and many are considered during all stages of the process. This approach provides a chronological description and provides the true picture of this process. Empirical studies reveal that process stages are easily recognized by practitioners involved in international business negotiations. Process development depends upon three dimensions, namely: time, issues and contacts. The more time a process/stage takes, the more conflict and distance is perceived by the parties. As discussed earlier, some issues, such as technical details, create a positive atmosphere, while others, such as price and terms of payment, create a negative atmosphere. Contacts are crucial aspects in understanding the negotiation process in addition to time and the issues. This factor refers to the people who meet during each stage of the process, whether on a technical or commercial basis. Technical people tend to stress technical details and specifications. Commercial people, on the other hand, tend to stress price, terms of payment, and guarantees, which tend to be more sensitive issues.

Stages of negotiation process

The *offer* is the period from the first contact between parties to the decision in favour of informal meetings. This stage indicates who approaches whom and how the marketer arrives at the offer. It also clarifies how these offers (buyers usually invite offers from more than one seller) are evaluated by buyers.

It is customary for marketers to revise their offers several times before submitting them to the customer. It is possible that the final offer does not meet the buyer's objectives, or that a competitor submits a better offer. In such a case, the negotiations end without any agreement. It is also possible that the marketer is summoned to the negotiation as part of the strategy (to create competition among sellers). In one such case, a government agency from Pakistan demanded an offer for a project from a British supplier. The supplier took the final offer after informal meetings and flew to

Pakistan expecting to sign a contract. He submitted the offer to the authorities and was kept waiting in his hotel. He realized after several weeks that the offer was demanded by the local party only to be compared to another submitted by an East European party, which the government had already decided to accept (McCall and Warrington 1984).

These offers and their evaluations lead to the next stage: *informal meetings*. Objectives (particularly the buyer's) and the technology in question are discussed to understand what the buyer is demanding and what the seller can provide. It is at this stage that the parties learn to appreciate each other's objectives and decide whether entering the next stage of the process is justified. Some amendments may be made to the offer at this stage. The process may end here without an outcome, or the parties may resolve most of their conflicts and come very close to an agreement with only formalities remaining.

Once parties decide to go further, *planning for formal negotiations* starts. They isolate the issues/points to be discussed during final negotiations. An agenda (contract draft) is formulated, jointly or by one of the parties. The choice of issues and the party who prepares the agenda is critical, since the nature and order of issues discussed influence the process, atmosphere and outcome of negotiations. The parties work at their individual ends and determine their positions on the conflicting issues. Third World buyers usually compare offers in terms of price and conformity to the rules and regulations of their government. At this stage, parties also decide on their minimum and maximum tolerance levels regarding different issues.

After all this planning, parties decide to start *formal negotiations*, whereby marketers are invited by buyers to their offices, where these negotiations are held. This negotiation stage is usually characterized by face-to-face communication and the use of different tactics by both sides – for example, persuasion, promises, threats and so on. Issues not yet resolved are discussed. Communication is especially crucial at this stage, particularly if parties come from different environments and countries. Communication can be complicated by differences in language and meanings. Although both parties may speak the same language it may be difficult to understand whether the other party is approving or disapproving. When both parties are using a foreign language (for example, Germans or Swedes negotiating with a Third World customer in English) communication is even more difficult, as these parties will differ in their language proficiency.

In the event that the parties cannot reach an agreement at this stage, but still consider it worthwhile to further negotiate, they may return to their offices and work on the conflicting issues. Hence, *informal meetings II* will take place to understand/check each other's position on the conflicting issues. After internal meetings, parties may arrive at new minimum and maximum points and their expectations are revised. Subsequently, parties may meet again for *formal negotiations II*. These formal meetings do not differ very much from the formal negotiations I stage, except that the parties are much more concerned to reach an agreement and are inclined to grant concessions. The negotiations are, however, held in the same manner as in the first formal stage. Atmosphere has the same function, although parties are more cooperative, and the level of expectations is more realistic since both parties are keen to arrive at an agreement. If parties cannot resolve their conflicts at this stage the process may end without an agreement.

Finally, there is the *implementation* stage, where the final drafting of the contract is considered. In many cases, writing the contract is a negotiation process itself. Formulation of contract language and originally agreed upon issues is a tiresome procedure. This stage is particularly crucial when both parties are communicating in a non-native language.

Outcome

The process of negotiation results in a certain outcome: agreement or disagreement. In international business negotiations the third alternative, a decision to continue the negotiations, is a distinct scenario. The transition from one stage to another means that the parties agree on certain issues and decide to continue negotiations in the coming stages. This outcome, therefore, refers to the final outcome of the process. The outcome, especially agreement, must be clarified to avoid ambiguities. Often, one or both parties prefer an ambiguously worded clause to allow greater flexibility in the agreement. Studies have shown that this type of contract always leads to greater problems during its implementation.

Chapter five

Planning and managing negotiations

Dozens of books have been written about negotiation, many of with which I disagree. I don't believe in negotiating through intimidation, fear, bluffing or dishonest tactics. A good negotiation concludes as a good deal for every one. . . . Negotiation starts with what you want to accomplish. Then the realities, and, sometimes, the complexities enter the picture. Sometimes many points of view and many elements have to be considered, but the deal itself must always be kept in view. . . . Your first step should be to rid yourself of an adversarial position. The reality is that you have a mutual problem, which you are going to solve to your mutual advantage. The intention must be to structure a deal that resolves the problem and gives each of you what you want.

It's not always possible, of course. When it can't be done, you are better off making no deal than making a bad deal. A bad deal usually brings a future filled with enormous problems. Negotiating demands a recognition of reality on many levels. Only amateurs try to accomplish something that isn't real or possible; it is an attempt that inevitably leads to failure. Amateurs tend to dream; professionals consider the realities of a deal.

(Nadel 1987:89–116)

In the past, the ability to negotiate was considered innate or instinctive but it is now regarded as a technique which can be learned. Experimental studies, empirical observations and experience have made it possible to grasp the art of negotiation. This chapter provides some guidelines for planning and managing the negotiation process. Specifically, the following issues are addressed:

• What factors are to be considered in the international business negotiation process?

- How does one prepare for international business negotiations?
- Who in the firm should negotiate?
- What characterizes a good negotiator?
- What is a good outcome?

This chapter deals with international business negotiations between parties having a problem-solving orientation, and not conflict- or game-oriented negotiations.

Factors to consider at each stage

The process of international business negotiations, presented here as a strategic planning model, is divided in five different stages, as mentioned in Chapter 4, and is influenced by two groups of variables: background factors and atmosphere (see Figure 5.1). Each stage is discussed in turn.

Stage I: offer

The offer stage begins with the first contact between parties concerning a particular venture and ends when the vendor submits a final offer. During this stage some negotiations take place and counter offers are made, often resulting in a revision of the vendor's offer. The dynamism of the process can be observed at this early stage where parties begin to understand one another's needs. It is important that vendors realize that in submitting an offer they are committing themselves to their part of the deal. It may be necessary to make concessions on many issues.

The offer stage is heavily influenced by background factors as well as atmosphere. These variables will often lead to an awareness of the relative power perceived to exist between parties.

In order to gain greater bargaining power, parties should gather as much relevant information as possible on each other, the operating environment, the involvement of other third parties, influencers, competitors and the infrastructure. Parties need to be aware that their relative power relationship can be altered at any time by such events as repositioning of competitors, or movements in exchange rates. To maintain their bargaining integrity negotiators must realize and appreciate the volatility of the environment.

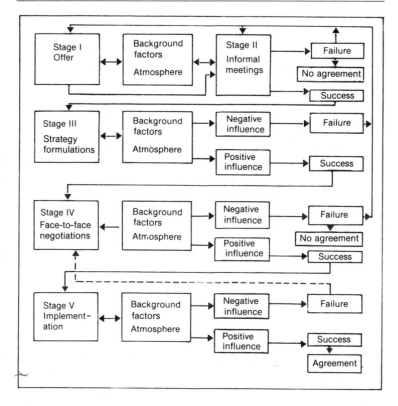

Figure 5.1 A strategic planning model for international business negotiations

Source: Ghauri 1986:74

Stage II: informal meetings

Parties meet to discuss the offer and to get acquainted. After the buyer receives the offer, informal meetings take place as the parties examine each other's position. Informal meetings are also influenced by background factors and the atmosphere, as in the offer stage. Whether the parties continue to the next stage of the negotiation process will depend on the perceived level of cooperation or conflict, power or dependence, and the degree of distance. The process often ends in failure if excessive conflict or distance is sensed, or if a successful future relationship seems doubtful. This stage may end with no agreement (end of the process), or the parties may start anew and return to stage I. If, instead, parties perceive more cooperation and high expectations for the future the negotiation process will continue. Success is heavily dependent upon the quality of the communication, each side's behaviour and expectations.

Informal meetings are often more important than formal negotiations in some parts of the world, such as Asia and the Middle East. Social, informal relationships developed between negotiators at this stage can be of great help. Trust and confidence gained from these relationships not only increase the chances for agreement, but also decrease the psychic distance between parties. One method of establishing such contacts is to invite individuals from the buyer's side to visit the seller's factory in an attempt to develop trust.

It is easier to develop such contacts if the firms have had prior dealings with each other. It is also often beneficial to utilize a consultant and/or agent of the particular country, to initiate contacts and to establish informal relationships.

Stage III: strategy formulation

Parties begin to formulate their strategy for face-to-face negotiation if stage II has ended in success and they decide to continue the process.

At this stage, parties try to build up their relative power. The buyer compares the offers submitted by different vendors, makes check lists and assigns pro and con arguments/competitive advantages to all competing vendors. The seller decides on possible points of concession and their extent.

A volatile environment can severely upset established relative power positions. It is essential that negotiators continue to monitor changes in the environment to protect their power position in this stage. A small US supplier quoted a large electric company a price in the customer's currency. He was asked in negotiations to accept payment in dollars, which he readily did. The customer had some currency fluctuation projections indicating that over the period between agreement and payment the dollar would weaken considerably relative to his own currency. Clearly, any relative power the US supplier might have had was diminished by his lack of knowledge of pertinent variables.

Parties must foresee and take precautions against predictable events in stage III. It is often assumed that information exchanged in the offer and during informal negotiations suffices for face-to-face interaction, but this is not the case. Remittance of funds, taxes and import duties, and work permits are just some examples of the rules and regulations of the particular country that must be researched at this stage.

An understanding of the infrastructure of the country and the company is also critical at this point. In some countries, especially when the public sector is the buyer, purchasing organizations issue a 'letter of award' (also called letter of intent/acceptance) after offers have been received. This document states that the order for the project has been awarded to company ABC, and ABC is called for formal negotiations. The vendors from Western countries often perceive this letter of award as a grant of contract. However, this is an incorrect assumption since other competitors might also have received a similar letter. The letter merely indicates the buyer's intention to negotiate further after receiving the final offer (more on this in Chapter Seven).

The selling firm must realize that the government buyer has different objectives to those of a private business firm. Objectives such as job opportunities, an increase in the capacity of the industry, balance of payments or other matters of policy will be dominant if the buyer is a government organization. This was the situation which existed in the negotiation process for a paper and pulp plant where the buyer was a big state-owned company. The right to reject the seller's subcontractors was reserved in this deal. The aim was to accept the offer which utilized local subcontractors, thereby solving regional unemployment problems.

As with the previous two stages, background factors and atmosphere are also important at this stage. In cases of negative influence, parties may go back to one of the preceding stages or, in the worst case, the process may end without agreement. In the case of positive influence, the stage ends with success and leads the process to the next stage.

Stage IV: face-to-face negotiations

The negotiation process is controlled by the partner which arranges the agenda, since it can emphasize its own strengths and the other

The party with the most information
will end up with the better deal

party's weaknesses, thus putting the other party on the defensive. However, the agenda may reveal the preparing party's position in advance and hence permit the other side to prepare its own counter-arguments on conflicting issues. Experience suggests that it is often the partner with the greater relative power which arranges the

When you begin negotiating, find points of
agreement to build a positive atmosphere

agenda. Some negotiators prefer to start negotiations by discussing
and agreeing on broad principles for the relationship.

Another way to ensure success at this stage is to negotiate the
contract step by step – discussing both conflicting issues and those
of common interest. In particular, discussions on items of common
interest can create an atmosphere of cooperation between parties.

Alternative strategies used in negotiations have been discussed
widely. A 'tough strategy' (Siegel and Fauraker 1960) is one in
which a party starts with a high initial offer and avoids making
concessions. A 'soft strategy' (Osgood 1959) is one in which
concessions are granted to enhance trust and facilitate negotiations.
The point is that to get a concession one must first make a
concession. While in a 'fair strategy' (Schelling 1960), negotiators
appreciate that a 'balanced' settlement would be fair to both parties.

The choice of strategy depends upon the customer or supplier
with whom one is negotiating. It is helpful to anticipate the other
party's strategy as early as possible and then to choose a strategy to

Never jump at the first offer . . .
or never disclose your last position

match or complement it. If both parties apply a tough strategy this may lead the negotiation to a deadlock. In fact, to enhance the negotiation process a softer strategy is often desired.

In stage IV both parties take the initiative by asking questions about the other party – aspects of the offer, price, quality, delivery and credit possibilities. These questions clear the negotiation range, or the gap between the minimum point of one party and the acceptable point of the other.

The negotiator should not agree to a settlement at once if there is considerable overlap between his position vis-à-vis the other party. The negotiator may obtain further concessions by prolonging the negotiation process. Negotiators who submit a 'final offer' up front can be at a disadvantage.

In view of the diverse culture and business traditions prevailing in different countrics, international negotiations inherently involve a discussion of environmental differences. It is very difficult for parties to comprehend or adjust to each other's culture or traditions, but it is important to be aware of these differences. Social contacts developed between parties are far more significant than the technical and economic specifications in certain Asian and Middle Eastern countries. Pride and face-saving are of great importance in East Asian cultures. Negotiators from these countries take their time and are very careful not to offend or use strong words; and the other party is expected to follow suit.

Negotiating with the public sector in Third World countries often involves negotiating with civil servants and politicians. These negotiators are bound by rules, regulations and government policy. Vendors must take these rules and regulations into account. When a large Swedish firm, Defibrator (the only vendor in the negotiations), offered to sell a pulp plant to India (Hindustan Paper Corporation), the negotiators could not understand why the negotiations ended in deadlock. The main reason was that the agenda prepared by Defibrator did not conform to the government rules and regulations. Deadlock resulted even though HPC's technical staff was very supportive of the deal and the Swedish firm arranged the agenda for final negotiations.

A balance between firmness and credibility is essential in all types of negotiation. It is important to give and take signals of preparedness to move from the initial stage without making concessions. Negotiators having prior dealings with each other can easily send and receive signals, but it is very difficult for those meeting for the first time. The timing of a move is crucial, but the attitude and behaviour of both parties can also play a decisive factor. A positive atmosphere may be developed by a negotiator who is firm and also exhibits a courteous problem-solving attitude at the same time. Negotiators from Western countries frequently adopt a tough attitude in negotiation which is perceived as a 'big-brother' stance and is very offensive to the other party.

Negotiators often send conditional signals such as 'We cannot accept your offer as it stands', or 'We appreciate that your equipment is quite suitable for us, but not at the price you mentioned.' The seller might say, 'I understand, but you know that this is the lowest price I can offer, otherwise I will have to call my head office and discuss the price with them.' This is a tactic used to test each party's commitment as well as the resolution of the offer. It is also common that the party perceiving greater relative power makes fewer concessions and that the weaker party yields more

You should read between the lines

often to create a better atmosphere.

Maintaining flexibility between parties and issues is of great importance in stage IV in regard to terms of payment, price and delivery time. It is necessary to make trade-offs (give and take). These usually occur after both parties have tested the level of commitment and have sent and received signals to move on. For example, price can be reduced if the party offers better terms of payment. Other elements can be traded off but there may not be a way to evaluate them in accounting terms. For example, obtaining a reference or an entry into a huge protected market may be strategically more important than obtaining handsome profits on the present deal.

A point will be reached when negotiators have to make a final move. The customer announced, 'The order is yours if you reduce the price by 7 per cent' in the Swedish/Indian pulp plant deal. The seller replied, 'Well, that is something beyond my authority. I cannot give that large a reduction.' The buyer said, 'It is up to you', indicating the final move had been made. In order to test further, the seller still insisted that he could not make that kind of reduction, and finally called the head office to preserve credibility.

It is usually a poor strategy to announce that the negotiators do not have the final authority to conclude the contract. But this is

I am afraid I cannot take that decision.
I have to consult my managing director

quite effective when used as a tactic to check the buyer's final move.

Stage V: implementation

At this stage, all terms have been agreed upon. The contract is being drawn up and is ready to be signed. Experience has shown that writing the contract and the language used can be a negotiation process in itself, as meanings and values may differ between two parties. In several cases involving Swedish firms and Third World parties, the language used and the writing down of issues previously agreed upon took considerable time. This stage can lead to renewed face-to-face negotiations if there is negative feedback from background factors and atmosphere (see Figure 5.1).

Discussion should be summarized after negotiations to avoid unneccessary delays in the process. The terms agreed upon should be read by both parties after concessions are exchanged and discussions held. This is facilitated by keeping minutes of meetings. This will help test the understanding of the contract, as parties may have perceived issues or discussions differently. This is helpful not only in writing and signing the contract, but also in its implementation.

Trouble may arise later during implementation of the contract if parties are too eager to reach an agreement and don't pay enough attention to detail. The best way to solve this problem is to confirm that both sides thoroughly understand what they have agreed upon before leaving the negotiating table (Kennedy *et al.* 1982). A skilled negotiator will summarize and test understanding: 'Do we understand correctly that if we agree to your terms of payment and repay the credit within three years from the date of the contract you will reduce the price by 7 per cent?'

How to prepare for international business negotiations

In this section we discuss the best way to prepare for negotiations and the factors to be considered at each stage of the negotiation process. Not all points are applicable to all international business negotiations; judgement is required for appropriate situations.

Identify the contents of the deal

The initial points to consider are issues such as implications of the deal, the interests at stake, the 'fit' of the deal with organizational objectives, and possible economic, political or other restrictions between countries. Parties should gather pertinent information as quickly as possible. What will each gain or lose and how important is the deal for them? What alternatives does either side have? These issues must be considered in terms of tangible and intangible motives.

Buy-back arrangements are becoming more common, and in large international deals buyers are demanding some sort of a product buy-back. The reason for this emphasis on buy-back is quite simply the lack of foreign exchange. Third World countries engage in countertrade deals to correct their trade deficits as well as to earn hard currency. It is important to calculate deals in monetary terms when conducting trade in this medium. The following story illustrates this point: 'A boy told his father that he had decided to sell his dog for a million dollars. The amused father gave his permission, and a few days later his son told him that he had indeed sold the dog for a million dollars. The surprised parent asked the boy if he had been paid in cash. "No", the son replied, "I traded him for two $500,000 cats" ' (Harrison and Saffer 1980:53). The seller might end up with goods which cannot be easily marketed in the home country.

The countertrade demand can be just a bluff, so that the seller who seeks to avoid the expenses of buy-back may offer a major price discount. The plant's output supplied under the particular contract is part of the payment in other cases. China uses its cheap labour and re-exports products from local plants to the seller's country. This is one of the objectives behind the 'special zones' policy adopted by China. Another example is the iron-producing Carajas project in northern Brazil. Most of the production of this complex is exported to Japan to pay for project financing.

Create alternatives

To negotiate effectively the marketer must gather information on the strengths and weaknesses not only of the buyers, but also of the competitors. By considering the resources and behaviour of competitors, marketers can develop their own alternatives on different issues. There are several strategies by which the seller can preempt competitors: (i) offering credit to the buyer; (ii) price reductions; or

(iii) long guarantee periods. Sellers must also allow for alternative solutions to conflicting issues. Question the firm's position: 'What if they do not accept this . . . ?'

Western negotiators believe they have only three options: (i) persuasion; (ii) threat; or (iii) concession. In fact, there are many alternative solutions to a problem. A problem-solving attitude is important, and it is not only a question of win or lose. Different issues can be combined to produce numerous alternatives. If the customer demands a 5 per cent concession on the price the other party can ask the customer to pay cash instead of the one-year credit proposed. Negotiators can also ask customers to pay 5 per cent interest on the demanded loan. In one case, the buyer demanded a 5 per cent concession on the contract price after everything else had been agreed upon. The seller instead proposed that he was willing to give a 10 per cent rebate on all the spare parts bought by the buyer during the next three years. This offer was accepted gladly by the buyer.

This point is particularly applicable to buyers investigating which alternatives are available in the market, the number of suppliers, their positions, and the differences in their technologies. Buyers must gather offers from at least three competing suppliers even if they have already decided to buy from a particular supplier. Next, checklists can be prepared for each supplier with arguments for and against each offer. Offers are judged on such characteristics as level of technology, long-term relationship possibilities, position in the industry, service possibilities, and on the people who comprise the organizations. This is the proper time to rank and categorize those issues which have some flexibility and those which cannot be conceded. By following this procedure the buyer can develop a comprehensive check list to rank the competitors.

Put yourself in their shoes

For negotiations to be successful, one party must understand the other party's position. This will help each side interpret and anticipate the other side's reactions to arguments. Anticipating and developing rational reactions to arguments allows each party to formulate new arguments and alternatives. This stimulates flexibility on different conflicting issues. Each party has to recognize the needs of the other, quite apart from gathering information and asking questions to check the other party's position. Being a patient listener will help improve negotiations. One can understand the meaning behind the words by listening attentively. One can create a positive and cooperative atmosphere in the negotiation process by showing the other party that he or she is well understood. However, be careful while listening – it is not what is said, but how it is said that is more important.

The harder a party tries to show understanding of the opposing viewpoint, the more open the question will be to alternative solutions. A universal feeling exists that those who understand are intelligent and sympathetic. Parties feel obliged to reciprocate in these situations. The other party will understand if you understand the other party. The ability to look at the situation from the other's point of view is one of the most important skills in negotiations. It is important not only to see as the other party sees, but also to understand the other party's point of view and the power of its arguments.

In one of the negotiations where a Swedish firm was trying to sell a project to Thailand a negotiation leader restated twice that the price for the Swedish project was too high. The Swedish negotiator, understanding that there must be some reason for this statement, promised to look into the matter by the next session. The Swedish negotiator talked to his Thai counterpart later during dinner and discovered that a Japanese competitor had offered a much lower price. With this information he was able to bring about a price difference in the next session.

Gauge the appropriateness of the message

The information exchanged must be adjusted for easier comprehension by the other party. Technical specifications and other material should be provided in the local language. Not only does this facilitate effective communication, but it also demonstrates respect for the local language and environment. In trying to sell a project to China, one Swedish firm presented all technical specifications both in English and Chinese. This was highly appreciated by the Chinese negotiators and created a very positive atmosphere. The Swedish firm received the order instead of a well-known American firm.

Westerners find it difficult to 'read' business people from other cultures. The problem of perception and language barriers often cause difficulties in the negotiation process. It may be difficult to know when they are angry, embarrassed or agreeable even if the negotiating team speaks your language. To illustrate, Arabs tend to speak loudly, giving the impression that they are angry, while Japanese tend to keep silent even though they disagree with you. This is frustrating and places an added burden on all parties involved in the negotiating process.

Cultural differences may cause difficulties in communication. Different cultures interpret messages differently. An octopus is said to have several arms in the United States. It is said to have several legs in Japan. In Sweden 'next Sunday' does not mean the coming Sunday but the Sunday after. In India 'next Sunday' means the coming Sunday. 'Nice weather' means sunshine in Europe. 'Nice weather' means cloudy or rainy weather in Africa and many Asian countries. The exchange of gifts and terms of reciprocity are quite normal in Asia, yet considered close to a bribe in Sweden. It is important that negotiators adopt appropriate behaviour for each negotiation. The chosen arguments should be tailored to the particular customer. One standard argument cannot be used throughout the world.

Barriers to communication also arise from real or perceived differences in expectations, which create conflict instead of cooperation between parties. In cross-cultural negotiations, non-verbal communication, in particular in the expression of emotions and the attitude of a negotiator toward the other party, is sometimes more important than the spoken language (see Chapter Seven and Hall, 1960, Argyle 1975 and Morris 1977).

Non-verbal communication can be telling. Liking and disliking, tensions, and appraisal of an argument are shown by numerous signs such as blushing, contraction of facial muscles, giggling, strained laughter or just silence. Whenever a party is negotiating, the negotiator must see and observe the other party. People, sitting down, lean forward when they like what you are saying or are interested in listening, or they sit back on their seat with crossed arms if they do not like the message. Nervousness can manifest itself through non-verbal behaviour, and blinking can be related to feelings of guilt and fear. It is difficult to evaluate non-verbal communication, as it is connected to the subconscious and emotions. The interior arrangements of the meeting also influence the

Watch carefully for changes in body language

attitudes of participants. A meeting held in a bright-coloured, cheerful room with flowers creates a positive atmosphere (Nierenberg 1986).

Effective communication and understanding of people will assist you in adjusting your arguments to the moods and expectations of the other party. Negotiators may continue to hold out, not because the proposal from the other side is unacceptable, but because they want to avoid feelings of surrender. Sometimes simple rephrasing of the proposal or a different approach to the presentation can alleviate the problem (Fisher and Ury 1982:29).

Build up relative power

Negotiators can determine who has the relative power advantage by gathering information about the other party, considering each party's position and developing different alternatives. They can try to build their own relative power by developing arguments against the elements of power and improving their own position. In the negotiation process, this kind of power may be increased by repeatedly mentioning the weak points of the other party: 'What happened to the project you sold in Poland? We heard that they had lots of problems with your machines, and there was some dispute about guarantees . . . .' The uncertainty regarding infrastructure and exchange rates must be handled here. Parties can agree on adjustments in the event of exchange rate variations. The party with greater information automatically acquires more power.

The negotiator may have to work as a detective to ascertain the buyer's needs, his strong and weak points, and the strong and weak points of competitors. An experienced negotiator can build up information for gaining relative power by being active in the negotiation process. This can be done by asking the other party questions.

Who within the firm should negotiate?

A difficult question arises regarding who should conduct negotiations whenever a deal is to be made in a new market. Who is the most appropriate person to hammer out a particular deal? Management must be wary of volunteers if negotiations are to be held in Hawaii, Las Vegas, or Bali. Those same volunteers may not be so eager to travel to Tripoli, Kiev or Beirut.

In fact, persons involved in international business negotiations can do more harm than good if they lack an integrated knowledge of their own firm and how different departments could be affected by the deal. Whoever is selected for negotiations must have a good grasp of the deal's implications. This is especially true when long-term relationships are being discussed. One way to minimize this risk is to appoint a negotiation *team*, whereby the key members are selected from the different departments which are expected to be affected the most. Management must consider team selection carefully as negotiators are on their own from this point forward.

The possibility of external help must be discussed seriously. It is particularly useful to take advice and help from outside consultants when the firm is entering a new market in which it has no previous experience. Consultants need not act as the firm's negotiators but they can offer assistance in formulating strategies or providing necessary information on different environmental factors. It is advisable to seek the help of a lawyer who has some expertise in the particular market. Most international business deals involve the application of local contract law, and the severe consequences of signing a contract entailing principles of which the firm has no knowledge are quite obvious.

It is important for management to realize that a selected person(s) should be expendable without creating organizational problems. When replacement is necessary management must be able to escape deadlock. These types of negotiations often end in an impasse and you may have to start with new players. It is also possible that the selected negotiators and the other party cannot reach a meeting of minds if the personal chemistry conflicts. It may become necessary to change negotiators in such situations.

When is your managing director coming to negotiate with me?

Key to deadlock can be to change the players

This discussion gives rise to another question. From which level should the executives for the negotiations be chosen? In most countries parties expect to negotiate with members of equal status. The managing director from the buyer's side expects to negotiate with his counterpart. It is advisable that firms match like with like.

This relates to a point made earlier – i.e., expendability of negotiators. The firm has to send its managing director for final negotiations if, at some point, it is apparent that the managing director or president is negotiating for the other side and expects to meet a counterpart. In Asian cultures, especially China, people are much more title-conscious. The Chinese CEO is always present during final negotiations and expects to meet the other party's CEO. In places such as Thailand and Singapore, where the Chinese community dominates the business sector, the CEO's role is played by the family's father, as most of the business is run by the family.

Parties need to consider not only *who* should represent the company but also the *number* of negotiators – i.e. whether one goes for individual or team negotiations. Team negotiating affords marketers the opportunity to benefit from the advice and guidance of many participants. It is difficult for a single individual to be adept in all kinds of commercial, technical and legal issues. However, the team must not have too many members, the person(s) selected must be able to take care of all issues and need(s) an integrated knowledge of the firm and its objectives for the particular transaction.

What makes a good negotiator?

A number of studies identify characteristics of a good negotiator. Ikle defined a good negotiator as one having a 'quick mind but unlimited patience, know how to dissemble without being a liar, inspire trust without trusting others, be modest but assertive, charm others without succumbing to their charm, and possess plenty of money and a beautiful wife while remaining indifferent to all temptations of riches and women' (Ikle 1964:253).

Empathy and respect for different perspectives are of utmost importance. It is not necessary to adapt or change yourself to local environments – it is more important to be aware of these differences and to show them due respect and acceptance. Asians and Arabs attribute great importance to social contacts and informal relations. A marketer's personality and social behaviour are of equal importance to social contacts and informal relations in Arab countries. Their decision in favour of a deal is often based upon the salesperson's personality and not on the quality of the deal (Muna 1980:30).

It is essential to know the negotiators' precise authority. In Eastern Europe and China, one team may negotiate one day, followed by a fresh team the next day. When this process is repeated a number of times it becomes very difficult for the Western firm to establish who is the negotiating party and who has the final authority.

One of the characteristics of a good negotiator is the ability to discover the timetable of the other party and allow plenty of time for the negotiation process. It is usually not feasible to expect to fly to a distant country, wrap things up and be home again in a week. Nor is it reasonable to coerce a party which is not ready to reach a decision. Negotiations with Third World customers take a long

87

It's hard to negotiate affectively under time pressure

time! Patience and time are the greatest assets a negotiator can have while negotiating with customers.

Some negotiators take their time, discussing all issues and justifying their role through tough negotiations. Negotiators must be in a position to change their strategies and arguments, as the process of negotiation is highly dynamic. They must be flexible. The other party will often ask questions, probing the seller's weaknesses, just to provoke and obtain more concessions. It is important to keep calm and find out first if the questions asked are relevant and justified. Negotiators can use this in their favour if questions are not justified and the buyer had wrong information.

A good negotiator is not just a person who can conclude an apparently good contract for the company or one who can arrive at a contract in a short time. A good negotiator is one whose agreements lead to successful implementation.

What is a good outcome?

A good agreement is one which leads to successful implementation. There are many examples of firms getting into trouble because they could not implement the contract conditions of a particular project. Therefore, in some cases no agreement may be a better outcome for the firm. A good outcome benefits both parties and does not make either party feel that it has a less advantageous contract. The type of arbitration was one of the reasons for deadlock in a case between a Swedish seller and a Nigerian buyer. The buyer wanted local arbitration while the seller wanted a Swedish or international arbitrator. The buyer's comments were, 'Well, if they are sure that they are going to fulfill the commitments of the contract, then why are they afraid to accept arbitration in Nigeria, because in that case there will be no conflicts and no arbitration?'

A good deal is one which provides financial gains. But what were the objectives of the firm when it decided to enter into negotiations? Was it the present deal which was most important or was it future business? The outcome must be related to the firm's objectives. If objectives have been met there is a good outcome.

A successful negotiation is not a question of 'win–lose' but a problem-solving approach to a 'win–win' outcome. The main purpose of the contract is to avoid misunderstandings and trouble in the future.

The agreement should foster relationship development and be flexible enough to deal with expected or unexpected future changes. Language and terminology used in the contract must be simple and clear. It must not be necessary to seek legal help every time the contract is consulted.

Chapter six

The execution of international business agreements

Joint ventures have been booming in Shanghai since China opened its doors to foreign investments. The following is just one example of joint ventures implemented in China.

The Postal and Telecommunication Industry Corporation (PTIC) of China, the Bell Telephone Manufacturing Company (BTMC) and the Belgian government are involved in China's first joint equity venture in software and semiconductor technology. The program aims to introduce S-1240 digital switching system technology to the Chinese industrial environment. BTMC's 30 per cent share in the venture constitutes its first major direct participation in a foreign company.

The Shanghai-Bell project is a venture with a high level of automation and in accordance with the contract BTMC is to transfer its latest technology and production know-how to China. The firm sent 120 engineers overseas, mostly to Belgium, for an average period of six months to be trained for this technology. The entire training effort added up to 60 man-years. All company documents are circulated in English and there are no language problems. The venture has been very successful and the company won contracts with 16 cities in 10 provinces for the purchase and installation of more than 40 exchanges with 150,000 lines. The technology transfer will doubtlessly build Shanghai-Bell's unique position as a pioneer in the construction of a technologically advanced telephone equipment industry in China

(Dai Gang 1987:21–8)

This chapter relates the previous chapters to the reality of general sales/purchase agreements, agency/distribution agreements, licensing agreements, and joint venture agreements. It explains the factors which must be considered in different types of business negotiations. The discussion is more specific with regard to different types of business, as it is difficult to generalize a negotiation approach for all kinds of businesses and customers from the Third World.

Sales/purchase agreements

Evans (1963) was probably one of the first to study the buyer–seller relationship. Previously, the behaviour of individuals (salesperson and customer) rather than the relationship between them was emphasized. Evans's basic theory stated: the more similar the parties in a dyad are, the more likely a favourable outcome, a sales agreement, will occur.

This theory of social exchange was further developed by a number of authors. Communication has always been one of the central variables in most of the literature leading towards negotiation and social exchange. Communication is involved in all aspects of the negotiation process and is often described as 'cooperative endeavour' in interaction. It takes place when one party encodes an idea into a message which the other party decodes, thus sharing the idea. The misunderstandings are often related to cultural differences in negotiation behaviour (see previous chapter).

Aside from social exchange theories, interaction among buyer and seller is of utmost importance to the process of buying and selling. McCall and Warrington (1984) reviewed past approaches to selling and concluded that these approaches did not consider buyers as active participants in the process of buying and selling. They discuss:

- The stimulus–response model, which argues that if the salesperson says the appropriate things the prospective customer will buy.
- The formula model (AIDA), where the salesperson takes a series of steps to attract attention, arouse interest, create desire and obtain action on the part of the buyer in order to effect a transaction.
- The needs satisfaction model, where the salesperson lets customers talk to learn their needs and then argues that his products satisfy those needs.

- The problem-solving model, where the salesperson analyzes the problems of the buyer and comes up with a solution.
- The traditional selling process, where the seller should be an aggressive order-getter and not a passive order-taker.

There is no universal model leading to better sales results. The buying and selling process depends upon a number of factors and upon the characteristics of the people acting as buyers and sellers – such as age, educational background, sales experience, experience with each other, and so on. The matching of buyer and seller characteristics and a positive atmosphere is more important. Perceived cooperation, power, closeness and expectations lead to perceived similarities and, thereby, to agreement.

Not all sales/purchase situations involve negotiations. There are situations where selling and buying takes place through negotiations, and others where selling and buying takes place through open distribution channels. The need for negotiation arises when there is something to negotiate for, and if cooperation and conflict exist at the same time.

In general, it is the sellers' responsibility to adjust/match themselves to the characteristics of buyers. Sellers have different characteristics and styles, yet buyers also vary in their characteristics and styles. Sellers must initially try to create a positive atmosphere, hence buyers will perceive them as cooperative and having the desire to satisfy their needs. Buyers see relationships with sellers as balanced or unbalanced in terms of power and dependence. In some cases they may be convinced to accept an unbalanced relationship. Buyers recognize less psychic distance if they perceive certain similarities. Finally, buyers must foresee long-term and/or short-term benefits or profits.

Other factors, such as the selling firm's reputation, its positive experience with the particular buyer or other buyers from the same country/region and its autonomy regarding price and other terms of the agreement, are of utmost importance, in addition to the seller's personal skills and ability to match different buyers. The more important the deal is to the buyer, the more attention is devoted to these factors.

Some authors (for example, McCall and Warrington 1984) advocate categorizing different types of sales/purchase agreements in a buy-phases model which is related to three types of buying situations:

- The 'new buy', where there is no previous experience and a great deal of information is required.
- The 'modified rebuy', where information and supply procedures are known but some changes are required.
- The 'straight rebuy', where there is a routine procedure to follow.

The seller needs to handle these situations differently. For example, in the straight rebuy no negotiations are necessary. Depending on the situation, different people are involved from both the seller's and buyer's side.

The importance of buying centres and multiple decision-makers must not be ignored. Buying centres as well as the negotiators influence a particular purchase. Selling hospital equipment might involve doctors and nurses, who are going to use the equipment, health service authorities, who have to allocate the budget, politicians, who have to justify priorities to their voters, and negotiators (hospital administrators).

UNIDO and OECD have published some guidelines for contracts in international relations. These are beneficial as they point out conflict areas in international contracts and provide guidelines for solving them. However, their usefulness is limited. Very little attention is given to Third World agreements. The incorrect assumption is made that when developing countries are involved the public sector awards contracts through bidding and not through negotiations: 'In most cases, in developing countries, procurement will be for public sector industrial projects and will be based on competitive bidding instead of on the basis of negotiated contracts' (UNIDO 1975:16).

In reality, no standard conditions are available for agreements with Third World customers. Though every customer and type of transaction involves different types of negotiation processes and factors, some degree of uniformity in agreements is possible. Empirical studies show the biggest conflict concerns whose law will take precedence in a dispute between Western sellers and Third World customers. Sellers and buyers want their respective countries' laws to regulate the contract. Hence, sellers need to clarify their position before entering into face-to-face negotiations.

It may be helpful to gather information on a customer's business relationship with other foreign firms. In Sweden it is quite common for firms to consult each other if the negotiating firm realizes that

We have to negotiate our own contract

another Swedish firm has recently concluded a contract with a buyer from the same country. They can ask that firm's advice and discover how they dealt with various issues. It is common for large firms selling standard capital goods to develop their own standard conditions, thus they do not have to negotiate repeatedly every issue. However, this depends on how homogeneous the customers are.

Another factor requiring standardization is price adjustment due to inflation. This is particularly true in deals with Third World customers, since delays are common. Delays can be due to different causes such as foreign exchange restrictions in the particular country, loading/unloading facilities at the port, or other infrastructural factors. A number of big firms are using contract price adjustment formulas, handling price adjustments due to increase in labour and material costs.

Agency/distribution agreements

Selection of an overseas partner is one of the most important aspects in international business. Most Western firms regard choosing an agent or distributor in a Third World country as the most difficult and crucial decision. Most firms start their operations in a Third World country with an agent or a distributor. A joint venture or a wholly or partly owned subsidiary is established after some time, after ensuring that there is considerable market potential in the particular country.

An agent and a distributor differ from each other in legal terms. They do not have the same rights or obligations. Agents act for their principals, who then enter into a contract of sale with the agents' customers. Agents in return receive a specified amount or a percentage of sales made as commission. Distributors act on their own behalf and, therefore, are merchant intermediaries. Distributors are responsible for the economic risk involved in the transactions. Distributors in return receive exclusive or limited distribution rights and accumulate profits determined by the purchase and sales price and their expenses.

A marketer's choice between an agent and a distributor depends mostly upon the nature of the product. Normally, firms dealing with consumer durables, capital equipment and products requiring after-sales service recruit distributors. Firms wanting to market raw materials and products with no after-sales service look for agents. However, the distinctions are not very clear in practice. An agent can simultaneously be a distributor for the same firm handling another product or for spare parts for the original equipment (McCall and Warrington 1984).

Clearly, a foreign firm requires a distribution channel to sell its goods within the foreign country. A local partner is essential to represent the foreign party and to engage in marketing and customer service functions. A mutual dependence exists in this relationship where both parties agree on some contribution towards the relationship from which both can profit. Parties have to go through a negotiation process to agree upon these contributions. This process is quite different from sales/purchase agreements since it relates to a long-term relationship where a certain degree of performance is demanded from both sides throughout the relationship. Conflicts can arise – for example, when agents are not working aggressively enough with company products, or when principals do not deliver on time or do not make the minor adjustments to the products demanded by their customers.

Western firms are used to different working conditions and are rather sensitive to the other party's behaviour. A large Swedish firm tried to negotiate and sell to a project in India without informing its agent in the country. The agent was annoyed. He thought that the Swedish firm was trying to deprive him of his commission, a considerable amount because of the size of the project, and tried to create obstacles during the negotiation process.

It is not only difficult to find qualified agents/distributors, but also even more difficult to terminate the relationship when a conflict arises or when the firm decides to enter the market on its own. The importance of the negotiation process is apparent in this case. The agreement must anticipate future aspects such as termination. The power and dependence aspects of atmosphere discussed earlier are most relevant here. Power perceived by one of the parties may have long-term influence on the relationship, with one party always demanding better performance from the other.

Western marketers must consider all alternatives to entering a particular market before entering into negotiations with agents/distributors. Costs and benefits related to these alternatives must be ranked in terms of control and economic costs and benefits. It is important to choose the alternative one can work with on a continuing basis and a situation where parties perceive mutual goodwill.

The firm must be very clear in its objectives, and negotiators must be aware of what the head office wants. It must gather information on the particular market and customer requirements to determine whether it will be able to sell its standard products, or whether products need to be modified. Different alternatives can be formulated and demands from negotiating agents can be better met if the information is available. A British firm was negotiating for an agent agreement in Pakistan. The negotiations ended in deadlock. The Pakistani agent demanded a number of product modifications to ensure market sales. British negotiators could not respond to this request; they suggested only some other minor modifications and additional incentives.

A distributor agreement can be even more demanding because there are certain investments in inventory, advertising and service facilities. An agent is not typically concerned with these issues. The distributor is also more likely to stress commercial aspects of the agreement, such as price, terms of payment, local advertising and service responsibilities. Western firms must realize that once a precedent is set (for example, the seller's acceptance to pay for service expenses or local advertising) it will have a definite impact on future deals. The distributor may demand even more generous terms at the time of contract renewal.

Building trust and commitment for a long-term relationship is particularly important in some cultures – for example, Chinese and Arab. Personality and interpersonal relations are prerequisites for mutual goodwill. Individuals from Western firms negotiating for such long-term relationships must consider the customers' cultural differences. While Western business persons cannot be expected to change themselves totally, respect for local culture and adaptation to the situation are essential.

Firm strengths, such as reputation, credibility, patented products and skilled negotiators, can influence the bargaining position of the manufacturing firm. Characteristics of the market, such as expected demand for the particular product, size of the market and number of distributors and agents interested in negotiating with the firm, are decisive factors. The manufacturing firm can acquire a better negotiation position when alternatives, such as opening one's own office/subsidiary, are available.

All this is related to the perceived power in the atmosphere and must be used or hinted at only when the other party needs to be convinced to accept an unbalanced relationship. It must not be hinted at when it can be perceived as a threat. Doing so will damage trust and goodwill. The Western firm can stress ideas such as its cooperative nature, its problem-solving approach, and mutual profitability in the process of negotiations to reinforce trust and mutual goodwill.

The manufacturing firm looking for an agent/distributor should gather information on its competitors already established in the market and seek answers to such questions as: 'Do they have their agents/distributors in the same market?' 'What kind of agreements do they have with local partners?'. A party cannot insist on 7 per cent commission if the industry's going rate is 15 per cent. Compensation issues may consume much more time than any other issue in the agreement such as terms of payment, the period of the agreement, termination of the agreement and technical support.

The firm must try to gather information on legal criteria regulating agreements made by competitors. Marketers ought to familiarize themselves with general country practices. In many countries – for example, in India, Pakistan and other former British colonies – it is possible to accept a third country's law. The firm must collect information on these possibilities during the strategy formulation stage.

Some principal–agent relationships exist only for a single transaction. This is particularly true in the case of project sales. Many governments in the Middle East insist that foreign firms choose local agents, even if negotiations involve a project from the private sector. 'You will not get far without a good Arab go-between' (Kennedy 1985:102). The right intermediary can help establish the right government contacts needed to get a decision, including a major project. Intermediaries may speed up the firm's paperwork, arrange for labour, materials, transport, storage and accommodation, and, most importantly, expedite payments for work performed.

It is advisable to negotiate the agent's commission up front, while negotiating the short-term relationship. This contract is often of significant value to the agent, since the intermediary can earn a considerable amount of money on a multi-million dollar project. Developing country businesses will haggle for this percentage and expect the firm to do the same. Commission must be tied to results and not to prospective business. It must be based on project sales and the value of the final contract signed and not on the offer nor on the amount the firm wanted to receive initially. Find out who the agents are and what other projects they have worked on in the past. Some may try to impress the negotiating firm by claiming valuable contacts and 'connections' in the right places. Such claims must be verified.

The tendency in most countries is to give locals 'a piece of the cake' and that all foreign firms should do business through a local agent. Relatives of the ruling class or families may act as agents in many cases. Firms must distinguish between bribery and commission. If the transaction is deemed bribery public opinion can force local courts to be strict. In one instance, President Sadat's brother was accused of bribery and sent to jail. The Lockheed bribery scandal revealed that an aircraft company had made payments to officials such as Japanese Premier Kakui Tanaka, Prince Bernard, husband of Queen Julia of the Netherlands, and Turkish generals. The Indonesian state company Pertamina alleged that Siemens paid millions of dollars to an official of Pertamina to obtain a contract to build power facilities at a large Indonesian steel plant. Italy's state-owned oil company (ENI) reportedly paid $130 million to a go-between in negotiations for an oil contract in Saudi Arabia. Recently, a German firm selling submarines and a Swedish firm selling arms to the Indian government were accused of paying millions of dollars to go-betweens to obtain these orders (Nierenberg 1986 and Schnitzer *et al.* 1985).

Rules and regulations on gifts and payments vary. British, German and Swedish firms do not have to be concerned about anti-bribery laws if the pay-off occurs outside their own countries. On the contrary, such payments are considered as legitimate and tax-deductible costs of acquiring business. The use of family, friendship ties and connections by the local agent or business people are customary in the Third World. However, similar actions by a foreign firm may not be acceptable.

Be specific while negotiating with agents about what they can and cannot do in the firm's name. Try to tie them to specific sales targets. The agency agreement must be cancelled within a year or other stipulated period if they fail to achieve certain targets. The firm does not need to exercise this right, but it will help at the time of renewal agreements, if conflicts arise or if a need for negotiations arises. The firm must motivate agents with incentives and favourable terms, since these are the only factors which would force agents to work harder for the marketer's interests.

Licensing agreements

Licensing agreements pertain to the lease of technical know-how, trademark, copyright or other intellectual property. Licensing involves access to that know-how and permission to manufacture and sell a product against payment of a compensation. It is a long-term relationship between the licensor and licensee and is often used as a method to enter a foreign market. However, competition may be created, in as much as the licensee is going to produce and sell the same product for which the licensor may have spent a lot of resources.

Compensation may be payable on production or sale. Some Third World countries insist on paying a lump sum in installments. There can be licensing agreements granting just patent rights, copyrights or trademarks. In the light of increasing nationalistic feelings of Third World countries, this licensing is considered most suitable for technology transfers.

The negotiation process for licensing agreements has more of a problem-solving than a win/lose nature, as both parties must benefit from the agreement. This type of ageement can be more complex because of anti-trust laws, the legal status of firms involved, patent rights, renewal of agreements and the obligatory secrecy during and after the agreement's expiration.

The first and foremost factor to be considered in negotiations is to compare potential revenues and costs with the expenses and incomes generated by entering the market through other ways. If the market is relatively big, what would it cost to manufacture and export directly or through an agent? Why not start a joint venture or a subsidiary? Alternatives should be evaluated properly before entering negotiations. Only after this kind of cost benefit analysis can the firm realize how important negotiations are and what kind of behaviour must be adopted.

After it has been decided that licensing is the best way to enter a particular market the marketer must gather information on the potential licensees regarding their technical, financial and marketing resources. A large and resourceful licensee can be too dominating and too difficult to negotiate with at the time of contract renewal and change. A smaller licensee, though less reliable, can be more aggressive in its marketing approach.

It is common for licences to be granted to partly owned subsidiaries. In this case, firms have to be careful with local anti-trust laws. In Brazil royalties paid to parent firms are not recognized if the parent company (the licensor) owns majority shares in the subsidiary (the licensee). Most Third World countries have special rules for transactions between foreign parent firms and local subsidiaries (Pye 1982).

Rights given must be tied to performance. Agreements must bind licensees to start manufacturing and marketing products within a specified time period while giving them reasonable time to acquire the capacity to start the process. Licensors must reserve the right to cancel the agreement (with compensation) if licensees discontinue specified business activities for specified periods (for example, six months).

If the licensee is going to use the licensor's trademark or tradename in some way, reference must be made to quality control while negotiating these agreements. Licensors must reserve the right to demand a certain quality and to exercise quality control at their option. In cases where the royalties and other compensation are related to production volume, licensors must be able to inspect the licensee's production and accounts. The party bearing the expenses of these control activities must also be specified in the agreement.

During these negotiations predictable future changes as well as unpredictable changes must be considered. The agreement may include a clause specifying that any unpredictable future changes which influence the nature of the business require renegotiation. Examples of such changes are the development of revolutionary technology, political disturbances/revolution or large currency devaluation.

Issues relating to research and development and further development of know-how must also be negotiated. Whether or not the licensor and/or the licensee are obliged to pass on to the other party improvements made is one such example. What if the licensee discovers a major technological breakthrough and acquires the patent? In extreme cases this can make the licensor's technology obsolete. Exclusivity and export rights granted must be specified properly. It is important to consider the future competition a Third World licensee might create through a competitive advantage such as cheap labour. The legal systems of a number of Third World countries prohibit foreign firms from imposing export bans on local firms.

Specifications regarding termination of agreements and the rights and obligations at the time of agreement termination/ expiration are important. Normally licensing agreements are renewed after the expiration date and, hence, negotiating firms sometimes overlook this issue. This can lead to litigation when one of the parties attempts to terminate the contract. Most agreements without actually mentioning termination stipulate that the licensee shall stop manufacturing and shall surrender all documents and technical specifications at the time of the agreement's expiration. In some cases, licensees demand to continue production and sale even if the agreement is terminated by the licensor. These issues must be discussed before entering into negotiations. The possibility of conflict is always present. What if the licensee does not pay royalties, or refuses to pay them at a certain point for some reason?

It is very difficult to give general advice for negotiating licences. Each situation demands different considerations depending upon the technology in question. Crucial issues which must be considered in most licensing agreements have been discussed.

With respect to negotiations, first, the question arises as to whether licensors should have standard licensing agreements or whether they should negotiate each case separately. A combination of the two is recommended. The firm should have a policy and a standard agreement for principal issues, and yet be flexible in treating each case individually. The standard agreement may be adjusted according to the information gathered on the potential licensee. However, the licensor must adjust the standard agreement before negotiating with the licensee. It is better to discuss and agree upon principal aspects in the early stages of negotiations – to prove and check the compatibility of objectives. The preliminary agreement discloses the relative power relationship and expectations of both parties.

Once a primary compatibility is established the Western firm must understand the legal and cultural implications regarding a particular licensee and country, and the attitude towards licensing as a whole. Pye (1982:37) quotes an official of one of the leading Japanese companies:

> The Chinese do not understand the costs of R & D [research and development], and since they do not understand the value of knowledge there will be big trouble in time. They do not want to pay licensing fees, they do not honor patents, and they openly say they want to copy what we went to great pains to develop.

Such cultural differences are important to recognize when entering licensing negotiations. The firm must appoint negotiator(s) who have integrated knowledge of the agreement's implications. People from different technical and commercial fields must be present. Legal aspects of agreements are of special importance and must not be ignored.

These agreements are of a long-term nature and often involve renewal and renegotiations. The agreement's clarity is important, as parties have to read and interpret it several times throughout the relationship. The parties must be very clear about the agreement's writing and wording. Both must understand it. It should be written in plain and simple language, understood by both local and foreign parties. The idea is to avoid litigation resulting from different interpretations. Local courts are not always objective when foreign firms are involved in litigation with local firms. Local courts may interpret clauses exactly as the local partner does. The local firm is in a better position to convince the court!

Joint ventures

Joint venture refers to the establishment of a new and separate organization owned jointly by two or more (parent) organizations. It has its own entity, and it is free from the financial and legal positions of its parent organizations (Pfeffer and Salancik 1978:152). Two firms jointly create a third firm for the purpose of doing business. This relationship is typically of longer duration than agency or licensing arrangements. The difference between a joint venture and a wholly owned subsidiary is that the latter is part of the parent firm and not a separate legal entity. According to Tomlinson (1970), four kinds of joint ventures can be identified:

- National joint ventures between firms from the same country.
- Foreign–international joint ventures, with partners from foreign countries who establish a firm in a third country.
- Mixed international joint ventures, with partners from foreign firm(s) and the host country.
- International joint ventures, with at least one of the partners from the host country's private sector.

Joint ventures are increasing tremendously in international business. Many Third World countries – for example, Columbia, Ecuador, India, Jordan, Kuwait, Mexico, Nigeria, Peru and South Korea – do not allow foreign firms to own subsidiaries unless they have a local partner. These restrictions sometimes even dictate that the local partner must have the majority share.

The significance of joint ventures is demonstrated by the fact that the People's Republic of China signed 930 joint venture agreements with foreign investors during the period 1979–85 (after the Fifth National People's Congress accepted the laws governing joint ventures in July 1979), and this rate is increasing. China signed 741 joint venture agreements in 1984 alone. There are several factors determining why foreign firms prefer entering a Third World country with a joint venture or with a wholly owned subsidiary. Unstable political conditions rank high among them. Economic risks related to the local market, balance of payments and other exchange restrictions, staff and financial resources are other factors. Staffing is very expensive and it is difficult for a foreign firm to import expatriates in large numbers or to recruit and control local staff.

A business enterprise in a foreign market is more complex to manage because of the broader area of activities and interests involved. Risks are greater for ongoing conflicts and problems in joint ventures. The problems are often the result of basic contradictions in the purpose of joint ventures as seen by Third World authorities and foreign investors. While foreign investors may view it as a profit-making entry into a lucrative market, joint ventures are an essential component of national economic development policies for local authorities.

Third World governments want joint ventures to achieve import substitution and generate foreign exchange. Authorities are interested in promoting domestic industries and often pressure joint ventures to buy raw materials and components from domestic suppliers. When a big Swedish firm dealing with household appliances applied for a manufacturing joint venture in the Philippines the government demanded that the firm buy and manufacture all of its components locally within a specified period. In another case, the government demanded that if the firm wanted to import components from outside it had to export as much to obtain foreign exchange.

Many studies on joint venture agreements reveal a high rate of failure and conflict in the long run. Kennedy, Benson and Killing (1982) reported a failure rate of at least 35 per cent. The high failure rate is related to the difficulties foreign firms face in choosing the right partner. This aspect has been discussed thoroughly under Agency/Distributor Agreements (see pages 95–99). An existing agent can be useful. However, additional problems can be created if the local agent wants to become the joint venture's partner while the foreign firm wants to consider another partner.

The selection of joint venture partners becomes an issue when foreign firms take the initiative and seek a partner, the local partner approaches the foreign firm for a joint venture agreement, or a third party brings the two partners together (Tomlinson 1970). Facilities and resources with respect to production plants, organizational resources, market position, personnel and local capital are considered to be the most valuable characteristics of a local partner.

The relationship with a joint venture partner includes a very broad range of activities and makes the negotiation process more complex as parties have to consider numerous aspects. The management of the joint venture is a crucial issue. Normally foreign firms prefer management contracts with joint ventures to gain control over activities. Hence it is possible for one of the parties to acquire more power in the relationship, even though they are mutually dependent. This imblance in the relationship can cause problems and conflicts in the long run. The power/dependence relationship is not static; it can shift from one side to the other. Experience suggests that parties in a joint venture consider taking on another partner for the purpose of gaining some skill or resource which they themselves do not possess. The relationship is of a complementary nature.

Some Third World countries have made it a rule that whenever a government agency is negotiating with a foreign firm for a possible joint venture it should have at least three interested negotiating parties, hence creating competition.

Again, information is of utmost importance. Western firms must gather information on rules and regulations of local governments regarding equity share, foreign exchange and import restrictions. Firms can use this to strengthen their bargaining power if allowed to import and sell in the country. (Since they will have the alternative to produce somewhere else and import the products into the country.)

The information collected helps firms formulate realistic expectations and learn how desperately the other parties are interested in or in need of their technology. In some countries the local authorities announce priority sectors for the coming budget period. For example, Chinese authorities announced four categories of projects as priority projects: energy and mineral resources, high technology, medical equipment and food processing, and construction. It is crucial for foreign firms to know whether or not these kind of priorities exist in a country and whether or not their project falls under such a sector.

It is important to determine whether the partner will be a government authority or an enterprise. The crucial issues are going to be different in the case of a government authority; economic development, employment facilities and balance of payments. Often government officials offer projects to foreign firms which are not feasible from a profit-making point of view. A private entity, on the other hand, is likely to have compatible profit-making interests.

Joint ventures are long-term agreements and require careful consideration of future possibilities. In a case studied by Hyder (1987), the local partner sued the foreign firm when it sold 9 per cent of its shares to a third party. The local partner claimed that, being a partner, it had the legal right to buy those shares. These kinds of issues must be considered during negotiations. Do the partners have the right to sell their shares to a third party?

Foreign firms are very interested in gaining control over the management's joint venture. It is not always a question of control but rather one of prestige for local partners. A Swedish firm had control over a joint venture in India. The local partner recommended a replacement when the Managing Director died, but the Swedish partner appointed someone else. This annoyed the local partner, not because the local partner wanted a certain person as Managing Director but because it was a question of prestige.

It is very important that the agreement for a joint venture anticipates all potential conflicts. In one of the joint ventures in India, where the local partner controlled management, the foreign partner was annoyed because of the appointment of the local partner's relatives to the key positions (Hyder 1987). It is better to discuss and include as much as possible in the contract. Conflicting issues must be agreed upon during negotiations; who has the right to appoint executives in key positions, who will select the Managing Director, and so on.

In the beginning it is advisable to start small and only to increase the capacity and scale successively. It is possible for parties to understand and adjust to each other. Otis Elevator Company, entering China, agreed on an interim joint venture before entering into a fully fledged venture agreement. The purpose was to effect a feasibility study of the market and to determine the compatibility of the parties and their resources.

To avoid problems with the local authorities, foreign firms have to check the responsibilities of the joint venture regarding the import of components and export of finished goods. A percentage to be sold in the domestic market must be agreed upon. The partner responsible for acquiring supplies and components must be bound to timely delivery.

Procedures for hiring and firing personnel should be agreed upon during negotiations. The perception of quality and performance of the partners involved must be discussed thoroughly. A harmonious joint venture relationship is dependent on the quality of the performance.

An important issue to discuss from the foreign partner's point of view is the measures taken to protect its technology and know-how. If the local government is the partner specify whether or not the local government has the right to use the technology and know-how in its forthcoming projects.

Contributions made by each partner must be assessed properly. Contributions by the foreign partner are usually more tangible than those of the local partner. Foreign partners provide financial resources and specific technical know-how. Local partners often provide management ability, local connections, knowledge of local conditions and land. No standard fee or rate is available to evaluate these resources.

Creating a positive atmosphere and displaying cooperative behaviour and good will are among the negotiators' responsibilities. Parties are discussing their long-term relationship – possibly even a life-long relationship. If no cooperative behaviour is found from the other side parties will hesitate from entering that relationship, even if there is compatibility in resources and objectives. A joint venture is like a marriage. Partners have to be sincere in their cooperation and adjustment to each other and believe that they will be able to live together throughout their lives. It is important that records of all negotiations be kept for future reference, mainly for the sake of maintaining the relationship's longevity. The agenda for negotiations must be prepared with mutual consent. It is assumed that both parties want the joint venture to function without problems and conflicts, and each partner wants to fulfil its commitments. Principles (objectives, policies and contributions) and details (assessment of contributions, rights and obligations, and day-to-day activities) must be discussed.

Patience is important. Time is needed by each party to visualize the influence of different clauses. This takes longer in some countries – for example, China. The time required to arrive at agreement can be even longer in joint venture negotiations. The Chinese want to put all the pieces of the puzzle together before deciding on anything. Foreign firms must not rush their partners. Taking time is to their benefit, as it is more likely that all the issues will have been properly scrutinized.

Sometimes the joint venture contract is divided into several smaller agreements. A separate management contract, giving rights of management to one of the parties, is common. Separate agreements to train local personnel may also exist.

The negotiation process in joint ventures does not end with an agreement. Conflicts will be present in everyday business matters, implying never-ending negotiations. Renegotiations may take place due to circumstances outside the joint venture. A change in political and economic restrictions may necessitate renegotiations. A new government or a change of policy may force parties to re-examine the relationship. Iran is subject to political changes. Mexico is experiencing economic changes. There are changes of conflict because of major changes in the structure of parent organizations – for example, the merger of one of the parent organizations with another organization which does not recognize any advantage in the joint venture, or unexpected nationalization of the local parent firm.

Finally, certain circumstances within the joint venture organization can force parties into renegotiations. In the case of an Indian joint venture mentioned earlier, the sale of shares by one party led it to litigation. Conflicts emerge out of cultural differences – for example, performance standards demanded by foreign partners may be seen as ridiculous by local staff. The concept of time is often different for a Western firm and for a firm from a Third World country. One week's delay in supplies may not be considered a delay by the Third World firm.

In conclusion, in the decision to go abroad companies ought to evaluate *all* possible alternatives. This can be accomplished with the help of a matrix, as illustrated by Figure 6.1. Each entry strategy

Criteria Modes	Investment	Cost/profit	Market- share	Control desired	Risk	Other considerat- ions
Indirect exporting						
Direct exporting						
Agent						
Distributor						
Licensing						
Joint venture						
Sales subsidiary						
Manufacturing subsidiary						

Figure 6.1 Comparison matrix for evaluating different entry strategies

offers a different set of advantages and disadvantages which can be traded off.

Chapter seven

Management guidelines

A business executive doing business in the Third World may find
himself in a very unfamiliar setting on an important business
occasion. He will have a hard time during negotiations unless he
knows the rules for proper behaviour. Failure is the most
probable outcome if he lacks cultural appreciation and understanding of these differences and behaves accordingly. Examples
of cultural differences are presented in this chapter. Here is a
quote by a well-travelled American business executive:

> I travelled 9000 miles to meet a client and arrived with my foot
> in my mouth. Determined to do things right, I'd memorized
> the names of the key men I was to see in Singapore. No easy
> job, inasmuch as the names all came in threes. So, of course, I
> couldn't resist showing off that I'd done my homework. I
> began by addressing top man Lo Win Hao with plenty of well-
> placed Mr Haos – and sprinkled the rest of my remarks with a
> Mr Chee this and a Mr Woon that – great show. Until a note
> was passed to me from one man I'd met before in New York.
> Bad news, 'Too friendly too soon, Mr Long' it said. Where
> diffidence is next to godliness, there I was calling a roomful of
> VIPs, in effect, Mr Ed and Mr Charlie. I'd remembered
> everybody's name – but forgot that in Chinese the surname
> comes first and the given name last.

There are no ground rules as far as the order of names is
concerned. Names are given the Chinese style but the Mr is put
with the given name in Thailand. The father's name comes first in
Spanish-speaking Latin American countries. The mother's name

111

comes first in Brazil. Roger E. Axtell advises, 'The safest course remains: ask'.

(Parker Pen Company 1985)

This chapter highlights the most crucial factors executives should consider while negotiating with Third World customers. Some of the characteristics of Third World customers, including Arabs, Chinese, Latin Americans, Asians and South-East Asians, are also discussed. These issues are looked at in the context of the negotiation process.

Travelling abroad for holidays as a tourist is great fun, but travelling abroad for business negotiations is a tough and stressful task. It requires people of special caliber and strong nerves. The Swedish firm Kokum received an order for submarines in Australia. A journalist asked the chief negotiator of Kokum on his return to Sweden if the negotiations had been tough. The negotiator replied, 'Well, you can guess from the fact that when the Australians announced that the order has been given to Kokum, the chief negotiator of our competitor [a German firm] had a heart attack and was rushed to the hospital.'

One negotiator returning from China stated, 'After signing the contract I was so exhausted that I went straight to my hotel and slept for three days.' A negotiator travelling frequently to China replied, 'a bath tub' when asked what he missed most while negotiating there.

Firms have to be active internationally in today's business world. They need to acquire negotiation skills to deal with far-away customers. The increasing competition in Western markets among Western firms, the saturation of home markets and the increasing demand from Third World countries for Western products and technologies are some of the factors driving these firms to Third World countries.

Issues never discussed in Western business deals are often the most crucial ones for deals in Third World countries. Let us review these issues: letter of intent, governing law and arbitration, time and patience, cultural differences, government restrictions, respect for the other party, and the role of third parties. This chapter will also be discussing issues relating to cultural differences and non-verbal communications.

Letter of intent

A letter of intent (letter of award/acceptance) is issued to the selling firm in Third World government projects. It means that the firm has been accepted as a supplier for the project. The letter is often sent after various informal meetings and upon receipt of final offers. Many Western firms become over-excited at this point and believe that the order has been granted to them. What they do not appreciate is that somewhere in this letter there is the reminder 'subject to further negotiations'.

In Europe, a selling firm receiving such a letter normally assumes that the order has been given to them and only formalities remain. In reality, the letter of intent simply means the offer of the selling firm has been accepted and the buyer wants to negotiate further. This letter is sent to two or three competing firms, as most Third World governments as a rule negotiate with at least three selling firms for a particular project. Western firms should not, therefore, expect too much from this letter. In one case a Western firm received this letter of intent from an African firm and, assuming it had already received the order, went into negotiations with a tough strategy. The formal negotiations ended in failure. The letter of intent must be considered only as a preliminary agreement affirming that the parties wish to enter into further discussion. The agreement is generally considered to be morally but not legally binding.

Governing law and arbitration

This issue has been a major source of conflict in almost all cases studied where foreign firms are negotiating with a Third World customer for the sale of a project, or for a licensing, joint venture, or agency relationship. The foreign firm, being uncertain and sceptical, may hesitate to accept local law as a governing contract law.

This was one of the main problems during final negotiations between a Swedish firm and a Nigerian buyer for a power plant. The buyer's comments were, 'Of course, as it is a Nigerian contract, the Nigerian law would regulate the contract. The arbitration, in case of need, will be done in Nigeria. . . . The foreign firm should handle the contract in such a way that a need for arbitration never arises.' The seller's view was that it was not Nigeria's law which was the problem, but the interpretation of the law which could create problems. The matter was referred to the Ministry of Justice, and the Managing Director of the selling firm had to travel to Nigeria to discuss the matter. In the end, the seller had to give in: it was decided that the local law would regulate the contract and arbitration would be carried out accordingly to Nigeria's law by a body from Switzerland. This body would be appointed to interpret the Nigerian law.

The same problem occurred when a Swedish firm negotiated the sale of a pulp plant to India. The local party wanted Indian law to regulate the contract and the Swedish firm was not willing to accept this. After much discussion the seller was told that Indian law was very similar to English law. It was finally agreed that English law would regulate the contract. If both sides are adamant in the choice of a particular country's legal procedures the prospects of a successful negotiation can be affected negatively.

Government restrictions

Before starting negotiations, participants must collect information on the rules and regulations of local governments regarding the type of business they are entering. Countries have different rules and laws governing licensing, agency relationships with foreign firms and joint ventures. Their rules and restrictions on foreign exchange and remittance of funds are other crucial factors from the investors' point of view. Rules and regulations about taxes and import duties must be understood by the foreign firm, otherwise it is difficult to negotiate whose responsibility it will be to pay these dues to the government.

However, it is not wise to rely on information supplied by the potential buyer. Firms have to collect information through their own reliable resources. Buyers will not compensate firms for wrong information. In one of the negotiations between the American firm and a Pakistani buyer there were lengthy arguments concerning salaries for expatriates who would come to set up the project. After some argument the buyer accepted the Americans' suggestions for payments (let us assume US$5000/month) to these expatriates and the contract was signed. At the time of implementation the buyer sent a cheque for US$3000 and expressed its inability to do anything contrary to the government's rules. The point was that according to a government rule any expatriates coming into this type of contract could not receive a salary of more than US$3000 if paid by local sources. The American firm had no recourse and had to pay the difference.

A Swedish firm sold a power plant to Nigeria and the firm faced great difficulties during the implementation stage. The central government refused to give work permits to the engineers who were going to install the machinery. This is a good example of the type of information which must be collected before entering negotiations. Such knowledge would have led the seller to demand that the buyer arranged such government permits.

It is not only rules and regulations which are important, but also the use of common sense to judge the country's foreign exchange capacity. Mexico and the Philippines in the late 1970s are good examples. Another example is a vehicle manufacturer who set up a plant in Turkey. The company faced great problems even though it had obtained the Turkish government's guarantee of sufficient foreign exchange. Unfortunately, the plant was virtually closed within one year because the non-availability of foreign exchange meant that it could not import sufficient material.

Respect for the other party

Foreign negotiators must never get involved in discussions regarding political systems and their inefficiencies, or any other issues sensitive to the particular country. Westerners usually arrive in a country with a 'Big Brother' attitude. They have suggestions for every aspect of life and how it should be reformed. Some business executives having been to India for negotiations a couple of times (for a week or so each time) argue that they know exactly how that country should be run!

Negotiators must always show respect to the people with whom they negotiate and for their traditions. They must not resent the behaviour of local people in negotiations, even if they consider them to be wasting precious time. This is a prerequisite for getting respect from the other side, and respect, like admiration, is usually reciprocal.

In Chapter Four it was mentioned that negotiators must attempt to understand the other party's arguments – 'Put yourselves in their shoes'. They must realize what is behind their arguments. Negotiators from Third World countries are bound to the rules and regulations of their governments. On many occasions they have to prove to their superiors or to the public that they obtained the best deal for their country. Foreign firms can help them achieve this, and they will find that this help will be reciprocated when needed. In one case, where a Swedish firm was the only vendor in negotiations and most of the issues had already been agreed upon, negotiations still ended in deadlock. The reason was that suggestions put forward by Swedish negotiators were contradictory to government rules.

The role of third parties

The role of governments in Third World countries has increased enormously during the last decades. The desire to be self-sufficient and the development of strong nationalistic sentiments are forcing these governments to control technology transfer and other commercial activities and to direct these activities towards greater economic development.

The advantages and disadvantages of go-betweens have been discussed. When entering negotiations it is wise to question whether or not help of a third party is needed. The firm should not hesitate to employ a local consultant or a foreign consultant who is an expert on the particular country. Some firms think this is an unnecessary expense, as they believe they can do the job themselves. Considering the many potential problems which can be avoided, the money paid to the consultant is a minor expense.

One American firm stated that when negotiating in China it always includes a Chinese on the negotiation team. 'They [the Chinese negotiators] talk to him in Chinese.' The Americans find the Chinese often open up to their Chinese negotiators more than to anyone else. Whenever they have a question, they always contact him instead of the negotiation leader. They feel much closer to him and thus disclose the kind of information they would never otherwise provide.

A Swedish firm was using a local consultant in Pakistan. The consultant deliberately sat at the end of the table near the opposing negotiators. He supported one or two of their arguments thus gaining their trust. Finally, he turned out to play the role of a mediator, and both parties listened and often accepted his suggestions.

The consultant does not always have to negotiate for the selling firm. However, consultants can be very helpful in providing valuable information on the country's rules and regulations, the

An agent can turn out to be a mediator

behaviour and resources of the particular customer, and on competing firms. Agents currently working for the firm can be of practical assistance in booking a hotel and providing secretarial help in the country.

Non-verbal communication in international business

Language can be a barrier in cross-cultural understanding. What may not be readily recognized is that non-verbal communication (also called the 'silent language' or 'body language') can also interfere in cross-cultural interaction. Non-verbal communication relates to the use of subtle signs, signals or cues in human interaction. Body language includes the value different cultures attach to time, space and material possessions, body movement, eye contact, hand gestures, friendship and agreements.

117

Time

Many cultures believe there is a time and place for everything. Westerners do not like to wait long! One developing country executive made the following comment about American business persons: 'You have one terrible weakness; if we make you wait long enough, you will agree to anything.' The timing of verbal exchanges is also crucial. North Americans usually find gaps or pauses in conversation to be disturbing, while people from other cultures prefer to leave a moment of silence between statements. Another point that must be considered is being sensitive to daily habits, such as the importance of extended lunch breaks in some societies.

Space

The physical distance people prefer to keep from each other varies among cultures. Showing close physical contact between members of the opposite sex in promotional material is considered unacceptable in many countries. In the Middle East or Latin America, Western business people may feel overcrowded, since in these cultures people stand very close, and touch and kiss each other. In these cultures, if you back away from someone who stands too close you may be perceived as cold, unfriendly or distrustful. In the United States, men and women avoid excessive touching, especially between members of the same sex. In Scandinavia, the conversational distance between people is even farther apart, thus giving others the impression that they are cold and reserved.

Material possessions

Giving business gifts of high value is generally not customary in the United States and other Western countries, while in many parts of the world gifts are not only accepted but expected. As far as material possessions are concerned, in countries such as Sweden and the Netherlands it is not common to show off expensive cars, boats and big homes. In other cultures, such as the USA, Asia and the Middle East, people may enjoy displaying their material possessions to others. Moreover, if invited to their homes, words of appreciation of such possessions may be quite appropriate.

Body movement

Studies indicate that when talking to a person one should carefully observe his or her body movements in order to grasp the full message. For example, if someone is leaning on the table and listening attentively this suggests that he or she wants to hear more or appreciates your point of view. Even the movement of an eyebrow can indicate a person's reaction. Coughing or swallowing of saliva often indicates that the other person is nervous or rejecting the idea. Moving restlessly on the chair also shows that the person does not approve of your comments and that he or she does not want to hear any more.

Eye contact

In many cultures people avoid eye contact when talking to each other. In some Asian countries, such as Japan and Thailand, people of low rank (subordinates) normally do not look into the eyes of their superiors while talking to them. In international meetings the seating arrangements are often such that the parties do not sit directly facing each other, especially if the distance between them is small – for example, if they are sitting at the same table.

Hand gestures

Hand gestures may have different meanings. The 'OK' sign (thumb and forefinger), which is also a symbol for 'made in America' in the USA, may have a vulgar connotation in some cultures – for example, 'you are equal to zero'. Moreover, beckoning by using one's forefinger is used to fetch dogs in Africa and the Middle East. Diet-conscious Westerners are complimented if you tell them that they are slim, while in some cultures heaviness is an indication of health, wealth and status.

Friendship

'Friendship' has different meanings in different cultures. In Northern Europe, for example, people do not consider themselves friends even if they have been working at the same place for several years, while in some other parts of the world, such as Asia, people consider themselves friends after working with each other for a short period.

People in Western countries are usually precise and wish to start talking business immediately, while in other cultures people are more used to informal conversation or 'small talk' before talking business. Asking about family and one's private life is quite normal in some countries like the USA and England, while an Arab businessman must not be asked about his wife, although it is necessary to have some 'small talk' before getting down to business. Several authors have pointed out that Arabs and Chinese are more concerned with the personality of and their relationship with the people with whom they do business than with the product/technology they are going to buy.

Agreements

The rules for negotiating agreements differ from country to country. In general, agreements are based on three basic rules:

- Rules spelled out, such as regulations or laws.
- Moral practices, mutually agreed upon, existing in society.
- Informal customs everyone conforms to without being able to state exact rules.

Westerners rely mostly on written contracts, whereas in the Arab world 'a man's word' is just as binding as a written contract. A written contract may violate a Muslim's sensitivity and damage his sense of trust.

Patience is a virtue

The previous discussion suggested that the concept of time is not the same in Third World and Western cultures. A European executive returning from Asia after several weeks of negotiations commented: 'As far as time is concerned their behaviour is very strange. We were told that the negotiations would start on Monday. When we asked at what time, they looked surprised and said, "Well, on Monday!" It was the same in the evenings. We could sit and talk up to midnight without any one showing a sign of tiredness.' There is no time for starting or finishing negotiations and foreign negotiators just have to accept this.

Official dealings in Third World countries take an especially long time. A foreign firm may have to wait several weeks before receiving a response to a letter requesting information from the central bank (for example, concerning foreign exchange rules and regulations). Official machinery works slowly, and papers or documents move even slower between different departments. Sometimes it is necessary to provide 'wheels' to make papers move from one department to another.

Experience shows negotiations with Third World countries for a major project sale take between two and four years, while similar negotiations within Western firms take between six and twelve months (Ghauri 1986). Negotiators need patience! According to Pye (1982), Patience in negotiating with the Chinese is based on the following assumptions:

- The Chinese must have time to receive and digest information they need;
- The Chinese bureaucracy is sluggish and slow;
- The Chinese have a long-range perspective and are not in a hurry;
- The Chinese want to avoid mistakes and want to be sure of everything; and
- The Chinese do not trust fast talkers who want to make quick deals.

According to literature on the Chinese and doing business with China, patience is the negotiator's most important asset. The Chinese take it very easy and check all possible implications of the issues under discussion. They do not want to make mistakes. They fear that they may be criticized later on and be blamed for possible future problems.

However, this characteristic is not only peculiar to the Chinese. Often, civil servants or politicians negotiate with foreign firms in those projects where a government is involved. They are very careful because of their responsibility to the public. Private enterprise negotiators are careful because they are going to invest their resources in the relationship and will be living on the outcome of these negotiations for a long time.

In dealing with Third World customers it is important to allow enough time and not to rush the other party. As mentioned in Chapter Three, negotiators need to prove they are tough business people going through a long and hard negotiation process. It makes them feel better. Foreign negotiators may often just sit tight and wait for the moment when the negotiator is ready to sign the contract. Western negotiators must be patient. They may have to endure much tiresome travelling and absence from family occasions and holidays.

It's hard to negotiate effectively under time pressure

From the other side, the delay is intentional – sometimes not because the opposing negotiators are being extra careful in evaluating your arguments, but because they do not like them. They are waiting for you to change your position. This is particularly true with negotiators from the Middle East. They provide hints and signals when they do not like the propositions put forward by foreign firms. Some foreign negotiators do not perceive or catch these hints and become irritated by the delay.

Sensitivity to cultural differences

Difficulties may arise in negotiations simply due to cultural differences. Misunderstandings result because the parties may interpret each other's behaviour differently. Good negotiators accept these differences and adjust their approach and style to suit not only the personal, but also the cultural idiosyncracies of the other party.

The separation of personality, political beliefs and social relations is very difficult in many Third World countries. Western firms must not expect that negotiators from different countries can separate themselves from their environment. There are certain cultures which are consistent and predictable. Chinese business people tend to behave in the same manner whether they are in China, Taiwan or Hong Kong.

Some 160 million Arabs live in twenty-two different states. They differ from each other in outlook, state of economic development, grade of conservatism, and traditions. Still, there is on the whole one Arab culture and behaviour found in all these countries. Islam is one of the unifying factors permeating the social structure of these societies. Arab hospitality is well known. Whenever a visitor arrives he is received no matter how busy his hosts are. They seldom say, 'I am busy today', or 'We can meet tomorrow'. On the other hand, Arab executives get annoyed when they visit their suppliers in Europe and America and are told that they can have lunch together the next day.

Face-saving is very important in many Third World countries. This is true particularly in South-East Asian countries and in the Chinese culture. It is best to avoid embarrassing or confronting them in negotiations. A Swedish firm was negotiating for a project in Thailand. The chief negotiator from the Thai side insisted on better terms of payment although his arguments were based upon incorrect information. The negotiator from the Swedish side knew this and promised to look into the matter. Later, when they were alone, the Swedish negotiator told his Thai counterpart that his information was not really correct and that the Swedish negotiators did not say anything at the time to avoid embarrassment. The Thai negotiator appreciated this gesture and became very helpful in future negotiations.

Cultural differences influence messages. Respecting the local language is very important. It is common to speak English in India and Pakistan, and all documents and negotiations can be in English without resulting in any problems. This is not the case in most other countries. It is best to translate technical specifications into the local language – for example, Chinese, Arabic or Spanish.

Respecting local culture and traditions is of the utmost importance. Negotiators from Western countries must remember that while they are negotiating, *they* are the 'foreigners'. They have to adjust to the rules of the game of this particular country.

In many countries, drinking may not be part of the social norm. It is looked down upon in the Middle East and in South and South-East Asia. Do not go to a negotiation session smelling of alcohol. Hence it is advisable not to kill time on a long flight or during lonely evenings in the hotel by drinking.

All Muslim countries have a special attitude towards relationships between a man and a woman. The negotiators should avoid discussing or being involved in this kind of relationship. In some Muslim countries one can be sentenced to death for adultery. Negotiators should be well versed in the culture of the country they are visiting. Many of the things that are seen as positive in a Western culture are considered very negative in the Third World, and vice versa.

It is advisable to be briefed on crucial characteristics of the culture of the country to which one is travelling. All cultures resent certain gestures or actions. For example, it is not considered polite to point at people in some countries. Do not cross your legs so that the sole of your foot is directly or indirectly pointed towards the other person in Thailand. President Lyndon Johnson made such a gesture inadvertently while visiting the King of Thailand. Nothing was said to him, but viewers reacted very strongly as the meeting was shown on TV. The President had not been properly briefed on the cultural characteristics or on the importance of the King in Thailand. A Thai executive commented, 'If we say that 90 per cent of the Thai people will happily die for the King, it is not an overstatement.'

The contextual background of languages

You need to know the context to know the meaning. Business people constantly struggle with ambiguity, as some languages are traditionally vague and people from the outside find it difficult to

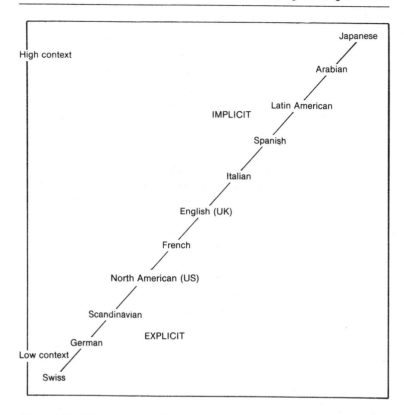

Figure 7.1 The contextual background of various countries

communicate. In fact, people from the same culture may also have problems in fully understanding each other. A communication expert from Tokyo estimates that the Japanese are able to fully understand each other only about 85 per cent of the time (Copeland and Griggs 1985:106).

Indicators such as, 'maybe', 'perhaps', 'rather', 'I'll consider it' and 'inconvenient' are some examples of ambiguity in conversation. 'Maybe' and 'inconvenient' mean 'impossible' in Chinese and Japanese cultures. Arab and some Asian cultures may also be confusing as they normally use over-expression. Their languages contain exaggerations, fantastic metaphors and repetition. When asked if they could handle a certain problem, they may say 'yes' without giving it much thought.

It is therefore important to read between the lines, especially in Africa, Asia and the Middle East. One needs to know the context of the language and culture to understand what is really meant. Authors like Hall (1960) divide countries according to their language and culture into 'high-context' and 'low-context' groups. Figure 7.1 illustrates the contextual background of various countries. It follows from this illustration that communication in low-context countries like Switzerland or Germany is more straightforward than in high-context countries.

Be cognizant of problems arising from translation. It is advisable to translate a message into the local language, but be careful of different connotations associated with various phrases. General Motors' 'Nova' sounded like 'no va' meaning 'it does not go' in Spanish-speaking Latin American countries. American Motors' 'Matador' suggested not only strength, but a killer. Ford's 'Sierra' means 'ugly old woman' in Spanish. An American airline in Brazil advertised its 'rendez-vous lounges', connoting 'a place for prostitution' in Portuguese. When Kentucky Fried Chicken used its famous slogan, 'It's finger-licking good' in Iran, it came out in Persian as 'It's so good you will eat your fingers'. Parker Pen's successful advertising theme in North America, 'Use Parker pen, Avoid Embarrassment' became 'Use Parker pen, avoid pregnancy' when translated and used in Latin America. In Persian a 'mediator' has a negative connotation and means 'meddler' – someone who is interfering and uninvited. In 1980, United Nations Secretary General Kurt Waldheim flew to Iran to deal with the hostage situation. Iranian radio and television reported his remarks made upon his arrival in Teheran: 'I have come as a mediator to work out a compromise.' Within an hour his car was stoned by angry Iranians (Fisher and Ury, 1982:34).

Western business people need to learn and adapt to these cultural differences wherever they wish to do business. What is even more important is to be aware of these differences and be receptive to local behaviour. Empathy and tolerance of cultural differences will often be welcomed by people as the most sincere of compliments and will help to enhance business prospects.

Chapter eight

Conclusion

Most people look at rural India and see only misery. Roger Little sees opportunity. Little is the president of Spire Corp., a Bedford, Mass. manufacturer of turnkey solar-cell module plants. 'In India there are 500,000 villages with populations between 500 and 8,000 that don't have electric power,' says Little. 'The cost of electrifying those villages the usual way – tying them to a national power grid – would be astronomical. And in India the grid is so bad that 40% of the power generated is lost in transmission. But give each of those villages a solar-panel system for its minimal electricity needs, and you're talking about $20 billion a year in business.'

A modern equivalent of oil for the lamps of China? Maybe so, but it's a dream that stands a good chance of coming true. Photovoltaics, the most advanced form of solar technology, is a market of the future in the U.S. But in the Third World the future is now. Solar-cell-powered water pumps and communication systems in villages and the countryside are a viable alternative to building huge new generators or stringing power lines across rugged mountains and burning deserts.

(Kindel and Tietalman 1983:126)

The developing world's growing debt to the West often makes headlines, but it is also a huge market for companies from the West, in everything from solar modules, heavy construction, aircraft, instruments and pollution equipment to communications gear. Some 100 countries in the Third World not only account for the majority of the world's population but, for many companies, they also represent the only growth markets available. While the industrial economies of North America and Europe, for example, recorded negative or zero growth rates in recent years, young economies of the Third World continue to grow at robust rates. Indeed, the inflow of advanced technology, improved availability of qualified manpower, ambitious development projects, and other assets have enabled faster growth rates than ever in some parts of the developing world.

Early in this book we argued that the market potential of developing countries must not be overlooked by Western businesses. Nevertheless, the unique aspects of Third World markets and customers require special attention and suitable strategies. Our objective in this book has been to provide the Western business person with the necessary understanding of the market environment and the appropriate management and marketing skills. Several differences emerge between the developed and developing country market environments. For example, government emerges as a key player in market regulation and enforcement. State enterprises also emerge as a distinct customer group. Government intervention in the marketplace also implies bureaucratic hassles for Western businesses.

Another observation is the dominance of sellers (primarily large manufacturers and wholesalers) in the marketplace. Competitive intensity is yet to develop in many Third World countries. Similarly, well-developed facilities for communication and transportation are relatively rare. This means that marketers need to adapt their product, packaging and distribution strategies to suit local requirements (see, for example, Amine and Cavusgil 1986; Cavusgil, Amine and Vitale 1983). To the extent that customers are consumers, their particular educational and social background must also be taken into account.

The discussions in this book also suggest that Third World customers are generally constrained in their ability to pay. This explains their desire to import technology and know-how rather than end products. Hence, the rationale for buy-back, counterpurchase and other forms of barter and countertrade is also provided. Developing countries are eager to attract foreign investment which leads to the generation of export revenues. Finally, the critical role of project financing and related aid arrangements is conspicuous. Those succeeding in bidding for large-scale projects are likely to be the companies most generous with credit support and creative with financing arrangements.

How then can the Western business person prepare to meet the challenge of developing country market potential? We believe discussions of this book provide three important lessons.

First, it is clear that one needs to acquire as much factual and interpretive knowledge about target customers, markets and environments. Familiarity with the situation and the players is essential to successful cultivation of business opportunities.

Second, it is also evident that what works in the Western world will not necessarily 'work' in the Third World. Unique approaches to negotiation, market entry and establishment, and marketing strategy are required for successful experiences. Several chapters in the book lay the foundation for an understanding of what adaptations are necessary and how Western business must go about such adaptations.

Third, and equally important, is individual adaptation. Successful management of cultural and social interaction with Third World customers implies that the Western business person must develop certain personal skills. These include cross-cultural sensitivity, empathy, tolerance, and flexibility. Among these personal traits, avoiding the 'self-reference criterion', our unconscious reference to our own way of doing things is key. We often accept our own culture and its ways as the norm and tend to judge others by our own standards. Our acceptance of our own culture tends to condition how we react to different behaviours, values and systems. In cross-cultural interface, sensitivity toward others is required. We need to develop empathy for other points of view and, whenever necessary, adapt our own behaviour. The importance of such skills in Third World marketing cannot be overemphasized.

We sincerely hope that this book has been rewarding to you in gaining an understanding of the Third World market potential and in how to go about tapping this potential. Let us hope that your actual experience in doing business with developing country customers is even more rewarding.

References

Amine, L. S. and Cavusgil, S. T. (1986) 'Demand estimation in a developing country environment: difficulties, techniques and examples', *Journal of the Market Research Society* 28, 1: 43–65.

Argyle, M. (1975) *Bodily Communication*, London: Methuen.

Bussard, W. A. (1984) *Results of a Countertrade Survey*, press release, New York: National Foreign Trade Council.

Cateora, P. R. (1986) *International Marketing*, sixth edition, Homewood, Illinois: Irwin.

Cavusgil, S. T. (1983) 'Public policy implications of research on the export behaviour of firms', *Akron Business and Economic Review* 14, Summer: 16–22.

Cavusgil, S. T. (1985) 'Global dimensions of marketing', in P. E. Murphy and B. M. Enis *Marketing*, Glenview, Illinois: Scott Foresman and Company.

Cavusgil, S. T. (1987) 'Qualitative insights into company experiences in international marketing research', *The Journal of Business and Industrial Marketing* 2, 3, Summer: 41–54.

Cavusgil, S. T. and Kaynak, E. (1982) 'Success factors in export marketing: an empirical analysis', in B. J. Walker *et al.* (eds), *An Assessment of Marketing Thought and Practice*, Chicago: AMA.

Cavusgil, S. T., Amine, L. S. and Vitale, E. (1983) 'Marketing supplementary food products in LDCs: a case study in Morocco', *Food Policy*, 8, 2: 111–20.

Copeland, L. and Griggs, L. (1985) *Going International – How to Make Friends and Deals Effectively in the Global Marketplace*, New York: First Printing, Plyme.

Cyert, R. M. and March, J. G. (1963) *A Behavioral Theory of the Firm*, N.J.: Prentice Hall.

Daniels, J. D. and Radebaugh, L. H. (1986) *International Business: Environment and Operations*, fourth edition, Reading, Massachusetts: Addison–Wesley.

Dai Gang (1987) 'Booming foreign ventures in Shanghai', *Beijing Review*, December 21, 27: 21–8.

Dohrs, L. S. (1987) 'Thailand: good times mean more bickering', Southeast Asia Business (University of Michigan Publication) 13, Spring: 20-2.

Emerson, R. M. (1962) 'Power/dependence relationship', *American Sociological Review* 27, February: 31-40.

Evans, E. B. (1963) 'Selling as a dyadic relationship: a new approach', American Behavioral Scientist, 6 May: 76-9.

Fisher, R. and Ury, W. (1982) *Getting to Yes - Negotiating Agreements without Giving in*, London: Hutchinson & Co.

Ghauri, P. N. (1983) *Negotiating International Package Deals: Swedish Firms and Developing Countries*, Stockholm: Almqvist & Wiksell.

Ghauri, P. N. (1986) 'Guidelines for international business negotiations', *International Marketing Review*, 3, 3, Autumn: 72-82.

Ghauri, P. N. and Johanson, J. (1979) 'International package deal negotiations: the role of the atmosphere', *Organisation Marknad och Samhalle* 16, 5: 335-64.

Ghauri, P. N. and Wiedersheim-Paul, F. (1982) 'Negotiations in turn-key projects', paper presented at the Academy of Marketing Science Annual Conference, Las Vegas, May 5-9.

Graham, J. L. (1985) 'The influence of culture on the process of business negotiations: an exploratory study', *Journal of International Business Studies*, Spring: 81-96.

Hall, E. T. (1960) 'The silent language in overseas business', *Harvard Business Review*, 38, 3, May-June: 259-78.

Hallen, L. and Wiedersheim-Paul, F. (1979) 'Psychic distance and buyer-seller interaction', *Organisation Marknad och Samhalle*, 16, 5: 308-28.

Harrison, G. W. and Saffer, B. H. (1980) 'Negotiating at 30 paces', *Management Review*, April: 51-4.

Heiba, F. I. (1984) 'International business negotiations: a strategic planning model', *International Marketing Review* 1, 4, Autumn/Winter: 5-16.

Hofstede, G. (1984) 'Cultural dimensions in management and planning', *Asian Pacific Journal of Management*, 1, 2, January: 81-9.

Huszagh, S. M. and Huszagh, F. H. (1986) 'International barter and countertrade', *International Marketing Review* 3, 2, Summer: 7-19.

Hyder, A. (1987) 'Joint venture relationship: case of Swedish firms', Ph.D. dissertation, Department of Business Administration, University of Uppsala, Sweden.

Ikle, F. C. (1964) *How Nations Negotiate*, New York: Praeger.

Jansson, H. (1986) 'Purchasing strategies of transnational corporations in import substitution countries', in S. T. Cavusgil (ed.) *Advances in International Marketing*, 1, Greenwich, Conn.: JAI Press Inc.

Johanson, J. and Mattsson, L.-G. (1984) 'Marketing investments in industrial networks', paper presented at the International Research Seminar on Industrial Marketing, Stockholm School of Economics, August 29-31.

Kapoor, A. (1970) *International Business Negotiations - A Study in India*, New York: Darwin.

Kennedy, G. (1985) *Doing Business Abroad*, New York: Simon & Schuster.

Kennedy, C. L., Benson, J. and Killing, J. P. (1982) 'How to make a global joint venture work', *Harvard Business Review* 60, 3, May–June: 120–7.

Kolde, J.-E. (1982) *Environment of International Business*, Boston: Kent Publishing Company.

Kindel, S. and Tietelman, R. (1983) 'Technology: if any . . .', *Forbes*, 29 August: 126–32.

McCall, J. B. and Warrington, M. B. (1984) *Marketing by Agreement – A Cross-Cultural Approach to Business Negotiations*, Chichester: Wiley.

Morris, D. (1977) *The Pocket Guide to Manwatching*, Oxford: Equinox Ltd.

Moskin, R. (1988) 'The Third World asks for a fair deal', *World Press Review*, January: 34–6.

Muna, F. A. (1980) *The Arab Executive*, London: Macmillan.

Nadel, J. (1987) *Cracking the Global Market*, New York: Amacom.

Nierenberg, G. I. (1986) *The Complete Negotiator*, New York: Nierenberg & Zeif.

Osgood, C. E. (1959) *An Alternative to War and Surrender*, Urbana, Ill., University of Illinois Press.

Parker Pen Company (1985) *Do's and Taboos Around the World*, New York: The Benjamin Company Inc.

Pfeffer, J. and Salancik, G. R. (1978) *The External Control of Organisations*, New York: Harper & Row.

Pye, L. (1982) *Chinese Commercial Negotiating Style*, Cambridge Mass.: Oelgeschlager, Gunn & Hain.

Ravies, P. (1987) 'U.S. investment in China's energy development: prospects and pitfalls', *Texas A & M Business Forum* 4, 1, Fall: 36.

Robinson, R. D. (1981) 'Background concepts and philosophy of international business from World War II to the present', *Journal of International Business Studies*, Spring/Summer, 13–21.

Schelling, T. C. (1960) *The Strategy of Conflict*, Cambridge Mass., Harvard University Press.

Schnitzer, M. C., Liebrenz, M. L. and Kubin, K. W. (1985) *International Business*, Cincinnati: South-Western.

Siegel, C. and Fauraker, L. E. (1960) *Bargaining and Group Decision-Making, Experiment in Bilateral Monopoly*, New York: McGraw Hill.

Smith, D. N. and Wells, L. T. (1975) *Negotiating Third World Mineral Agreements*, Cambridge, Mass.: Ballinger.

Tefft, S., Javetski, B. and Pitzer, M. J. (1987) 'Why the U.S. is trying harder to make friends with India', *Business Week*, 12 January: 61.

Tomlinson, J. W. C. (1970) *The Joint Venture Process in International Business: India and Pakistan*, Cambridge Mass., the M.I.T. Press.

Tung, R. L. (1982) 'US–China trade negotiations', *Journal of International Business Studies*, Fall: 25–38.

UNIDO (1975) *Guidelines for Contracting for Industrial Projects in Developing Countries*, E.75.II.B.3., New York: 47–58.

World Bank (1985) *SRI Highlights, Joint Ventures in PRC*, World Business Division Publication.

Yearbook for Trade Statistics (1978) New York: United Nations.

Index